WOODWORK

An illustrated
Teach Yourself book

Alfred Yarwood

Illustrated Teach Yourself **Woodwork**

TREASURE PRESS

First published in Great Britain in 1978 by Hodder and Stoughton Ltd

This edition published in 1984 by
Treasure Press
59 Grosvenor Street
London W1

Text © 1978 Alfred Yarwood
Illustrations © 1978 Alfred Yarwood

ISBN 0 907812 55 4

Printed in Hong Kong

Contents

1 Wood

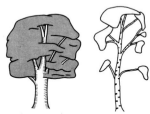

fig 1: 'broad-leaved' hardwood trees, beech and birch

fig 2: broad leaves, beech and
birch

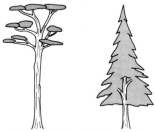

fig 3: 'softwood' trees, Scots
pine and spruce

fig 4: needle-shaped leaves,
Scots pine and spruce

Wood is a remarkable material. Its main value lies in the fact
that, if for every tree felled to produce timber, another tree is
planted to replace it, there will always be sufficient timber
for our purposes. Wood is a material which is relatively easy
to work to shape, yet is tough and strong; it possesses
variations of beauty which other materials lack; it is easily
available from a large number of suppliers; it is relatively
cheap. It is one of the few constructional materials which
can be worked at home without the need to purchase
expensive machinery. It can be worked if necessary with
only a few tools.

Many hundreds of different species of trees are sawn into
timbers from which woodworkers make a vast range of
articles. There is a timber-producing industry in the British
Isles, but most of the timber used in the British Isles is
imported from countries all over the world — building
timbers from Canada, Russia, the Baltic; furniture timbers
from Africa, South America, the U.S.A., Japan; teak and
ebony from Burma and India; Parana pine from Brazil;
special timbers from Australia. There is hardly a country in
the world which does not engage in this trade.

Hardwoods and softwoods

Woodworkers classify woods into two types — hardwoods
and softwoods. Hardwoods are from trees with broad
leaves — oak, ash, beech, mahogany, teak. Softwoods are
from coniferous trees — larch, red deal (Scots pine), spruce.
Nearly all 'hardwoods' are harder than 'softwoods' but there
are a few exceptions. Balsa, which is very soft and very light
in weight, is a 'hardwood' to a woodworker because it is
obtained from a broad-leaved tree. Balsa grows in the
tropical parts of the Americas and in Ceylon. Pitch pine on
the other hand is a 'softwood' despite its being very hard
and difficult to work, because the pitch pine tree is
coniferous.

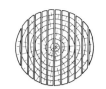

fig 5: sawing a log by slash sawing

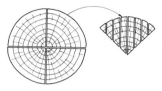

fig 6: sawing a log by quarter sawing

fig 7: a 'warped' slash-sawn board

fig 8: quarter-sawn boards remain flat

Processes of producing wood

The wood from which you will be making various articles is the result of a series of processes. First the tree must be felled. The branches and twigs are then sawn or axed from the main tree trunk. The resulting log is transported to a saw mill by lorry, train, ship or by floating down rivers. The log is sawn into boards at a saw mill. These boards must then be dried or 'seasoned' before they are suitable for the making of wooden articles.

Sawing of logs into boards

Two principal methods of sawing logs into boards are by 'slash' sawing or 'quarter' sawing. Quarter-sawn boards are more expensive to produce than slash-sawn boards but have the advantage of showing good quality 'figure' and of remaining flat and not 'warping'.

Seasoning

Two methods of seasoning are commonly practised — open-air seasoning and kiln seasoning. Kilns are similar to giant ovens in which temperature and moisture are closely controlled to allow timber to be dried in six or seven weeks. Open-air seasoning is a longer process taking up to a year or even longer. You will probably have seen stacks of timber being seasoned when you have been travelling by car or in a train. Notice the careful, orderly stacking with 'piling sticks' to allow circulation of air. Wet (or 'green') timber cannot be worked because tools will simply not cut such wood; it cannot be painted or polished because paints or polishes peel off the wet surfaces; it warps, twists and splits easily; it is heavier but weaker than seasoned timber.

Purchasing wood

When you wish to buy wood, it is best, if possible, to go to a timber yard. There are often several in most towns. Most of the people who run these yards will sell to you either small or large quantities of wood and will often show much interest in what you are making. The second source of supply is from 'do-it-yourself' shops, where small or large pieces of wood can be easily purchased. In some you can select the actual pieces you wish to buy. However these shops rarely carry the same variety of timbers as do timber yards. If you are still at school, your woodwork teacher might allow you to buy pieces of wood from the school, particularly if he knows of your interest in the subject. Adults attending evening classes in woodwork can usually purchase wood from the teacher or instructor.

Waste wood from buildings being demolished or from cupboards and fittings being replaced is a good source of supply. Second-hand timber is often free for the asking and can be of very good quality, but all nails and screws should be removed and polish or paint scraped off. Many people think wood is expensive, but this is not so if you shop around. Prices vary considerably among shops so it is advisable to look at prices elsewhere before you buy from any particular shop.

Types of wood on the market

Boards planed both sides (PBS) can be purchased in thicknesses finishing 6 mm; 10 mm; 15 mm; 20 mm; 22 mm or thicker. Such boards vary in width from about 150 mm up to a maximum of about 300 mm. Strips of wood planed all round (PAR) of various sectional dimensions are often carried in stock sizes. Common sizes are — 45 mm by 22 mm; 70 mm by 15 mm; 90 mm by 13 mm. Common strip 'squares' are 22 mm square; 35 mm square; 45 mm square.

Manufactured boards are often easier to purchase than 'solid' wood. They have the following advantages: good quality; they do not shrink or expand when included in constructions; they can be purchased with a variety of face veneers. A common manufactured board is hardboard sold in sheets up to 2400 mm by 1200 mm and of 3 mm or 6 mm thickness. Plywoods are made from various woods, of differing thicknesses and in small or large boards. A common thickness is 3 mm 3 ply, but 4 mm 3 ply, 6 mm 5 ply, 9 mm 5 ply and others can be obtained. Blockboards 15 mm, 18 mm or 22 mm thick are available with a choice of facings. Chipboards — 15 mm and 18 mm thicknesses — are common and can be bought either unfaced or faced with wood or plastic veneers.

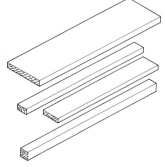

fig 9: boards, strips and squares

Woods available

The common building wood is Scots pine. It is never called this but is referred to as red deal, redwood or even as yellow deal. It is a strong softwood. The most easily obtainable hardwoods are African mahogany — a rich pink brown; Ramin — straight grained and a uniform straw colour; Utile — light pink brown without a distinct grain; Afrormosia — deep brown with good grain; Teak — rich dark brown, one of the best of all timbers but very expensive. You may find you can purchase woods such as Oak, which is a light straw brown colour with good grain and a 'flash' figure; Ash — a very

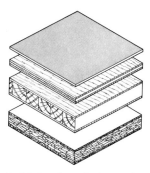

fig 10: hardboard, plywood, blockboard and chipboard

Cutting a housing groove.
See page 34

tough wood with a pronounced grain marking — and others.

Plywoods, chipboards and blockboards can be purchased with mahogany, teak, afrormosia, oak or walnut-veneered faces. Chipboard is also available with white vinyl or melamine (plastics) faces or with imitation wood faces made from vinyl or melamine sheet.

Table — afrormosia frame and
tiled top. See page 89

2 Tools and equipment

Building up a tool kit

When starting woodwork as a hobby, it is best to build up a tool kit as interest and knowledge of working in wood progresses. Tools are expensive. Some words of advice when purchasing tools may therefore be needed. Always buy the best you can afford at the time of purchase. Well-made hand tools will give good, constant service for many years and will often last a lifetime. Before buying any tool, look around the shops to see what is available. Compare designs. Compare costs. Handle the tool. Does it feel well-balanced? Is it comfortable to hold and handle? Is it made by a firm of good repute? Is it the right size? Is it exactly what you are looking for? If you add to your kit of woodworking tools as you gain experience, the resulting collection will be better suited to your needs than if all the tools are purchased at one time. Knowledge about tools comes with handling and using them. Part of that experience is concerned with buying them. There is the enjoyment gained from looking around for the tools best suited to your requirements, saving up for their cost and in gradually building up what, for you, is the perfect kit. It is all part of the interest of woodworking.

fig 11: firmer chisel, plastic handled, 18 mm wide blade

fig 12: firmer chisel, wood handled, 18 mm wide blade

You could make a beginning with three essential tools. A handsaw and two 'firmer' chisels. A suitable general-purpose handsaw would be one with a 500 mm long blade, with medium-size saw teeth. Two firmer chisels of 6 mm and 25 mm blade widths will be suitable. These three tools alone will allow you to do a great deal of work in wood. The next tool you will probably need is a hammer for driving nails and for assembling work. A good first hammer would be a claw type. When a few nailed constructions have been built, you may find you need a plane for cleaning rough surfaces. A smoothing plane is a good buy. It is a good, general-purpose tool with which most planing jobs can be tackled. A small collection of screwdrivers will soon be required. Not only will the possession of these allow you to

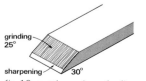

fig 13: cutting edge of a firmer chisel

grinding 25°

sharpening 30°

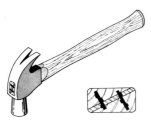

fig 14: a claw hammer, 750 gram head

fig 15: carpenter's hammer, 500 gram head

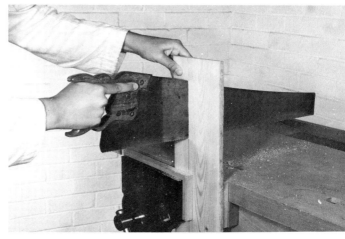

'Ripping' with a handsaw

fig 16: smoothing plane, 220 mm long with 50 mm cutting blade

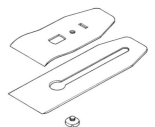

fig 17: cutting blade and cap iron from plane

fig 18: cutting blade and cap iron assembled

Right: removing a bent nail with a claw hammer

13

Shavings produced by a well-sharpened plane

assemble screwed constructions, but they will also enable you to fix fittings such as handles and hinges.

Some form of ruler for measuring will quickly become essential, as will a try square. Try squares are for 'squaring' lines at 90 degrees across wood and for testing whether parts have been assembled 'square'.

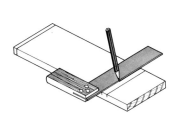

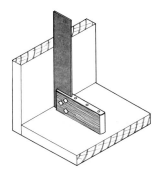

fig 19: try square, 150 mm blade

fig 20: squaring a line across wood

fig 21: testing a corner with try square

By now the list of tools in the kit is becoming quite impressive. With this basic kit — handsaw, two chisels, hammer, plane, some screwdrivers, a ruler and a try square — you can attempt a large variety of projects in wood.

Now take a look at other tools which can be purchased as the need arises and when you have the money. The following are suggestions for additional tools listed in a rough order of importance.

Opposite: sawing a curved line with a coping saw

fig 22: a mortise chisel, 6 mm wide blade

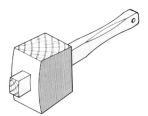

fig 23: carpenter's mallet

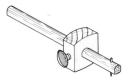

fig 24: marking gauge

Six firmer chisels — 3 mm; 6 mm; 13 mm; 15 mm; 18 mm and 25 mm widths — will cater for all chiselling. Useful additional chisels are mortise chisels, preferably with wooden (boxwood) handles. Boxwood handles will allow the chisels to be struck repeatedly by a mallet without damage to the mallet faces. Two widths of mortise chisel — 6 mm and 9 mm — will cover most of the work for which mortise chisels are designed. A mallet might be regarded as a necessity. The standard carpenter's beech mallet would be an excellent choice. Additional saws are an aid to good working, particularly a tenon saw of about 250 mm blade length for finer sawing than the handsaw. A coping saw is an additional saw for curved work. Another tool for shaping is a Surform tool. A marking gauge makes the marking of lines parallel to edges easy and precise. A pair of pincers for pulling out nails and for cutting wire can be of value. To complete a first-rate, all-round tool kit, some tools for boring and drilling holes are advisable. A carpenter's brace, with 'bits' purchased as required and a hand drill with some drills. Possibly, at a later stage, you might consider buying that very versatile modern tool — a power drill.

This list by no means exhausts the tools you can purchase for working in wood, but if you are fortunate enough to possess all the tools listed you can tackle a very wide range of projects. A few other tools will be mentioned in later pages. If you become very interested in this craft, there are many other tools you may like to possess. There is a wide range of planes for special purposes; a variety of saws; tools such as gouges in bewildering array for woodcarving; specialised marking tools; the list is almost endless. These more advanced tools are, however, beyond the scope of this book.

Boring a hole with a brace

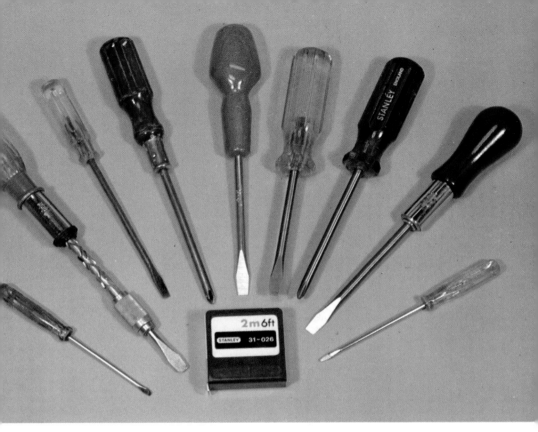

A selection of screwdrivers

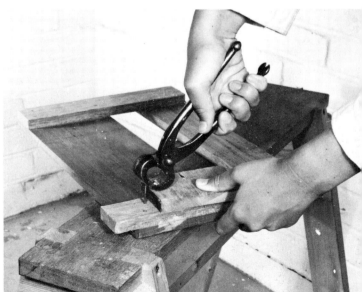

Removing a bent nail with a pair of pincers

Maintenance and sharpening

To obtain the best service from woodworking tools they need to be maintained in a clean and sharp condition. Badly maintained or blunt tools do not work as well as they should and can even be a source of danger. For example a blunt tool can slip instead of cutting the line along which it is being worked. Pride in the quality of the maintenance of tools leads to pride in the quality of the work made with them.

Where should tools be stored? They can be kept in boxes, or in racks, in drawers or in cupboards. Wherever they are stored that place should be set aside for nothing but tools. If you are fortunate in possessing a special place in which to practise woodworking – a shed, or a room or even a special workshop – you will find the best method of storage is to make individual racks for each tool. Such racks can be made from wood, although there are various clips and holders which can be purchased for the purpose. If your woodworking must be carried out in any space available at the time, the best storage method is possibly to make, or to purchase, a tool box which can be carried from place to place. Woodwork tools do not take kindly to metal tool boxes – wooden boxes are preferable. Moisture is an enemy to good tool maintenance. It makes rust form on the surfaces of most tool steels. Rusting can be prevented by placing bags of silica gel crystals or strips of rust-inhibiting paper between tools. No matter how you store your tools, make it a rule to make sure that all tools are cleaned and put away in their proper places at the end of a session of woodworking. Waste such as sawdust and chips should be swept up.

fig 25: tool box for woodwork tools

Woodwork tools stored in a fitted cupboard

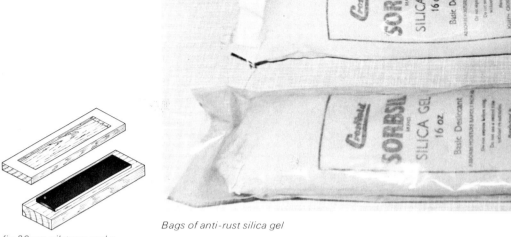
Bags of anti-rust silica gel

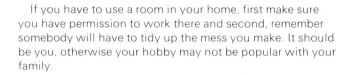
fig 26: an oilstone and a wooden case

fig 27: directions of movement of blades over oilstone when sharpening

fig 28: a burr or 'wire edge' raised on back of edge being sharpened

If you have to use a room in your home, first make sure you have permission to work there and second, remember somebody will have to tidy up the mess you make. It should be you, otherwise your hobby may not be popular with your family.

Sharpening edge tools

The cutting edges of plane blades and chisels will require sharpening at fairly frequent intervals of time. The method is as follows. Drip thin lubricating oil on to the surface of an oilstone. Hold the chisel or blade at an angle of about 30 degrees to the surface of the stone and work the cutting edge along and over its surface applying firm pressure downwards with the hands. A sharpening or 'honing' guide helps to obtain an accurate angle, but such a device is not essential. Continue working the blade over the stone until a burr or 'wire edge' forms on the back of the blade. Now turn the blade right over and, holding it quite flat, rub it over the surface of the stone. These two operations, first at 30 degrees and then reversing to flat, may need to be repeated several times to weaken the burr. The burr is removed by pushing the sharpened edge firmly into a piece of softwood. The oilstone should then be cleaned with waste rag before being put away.

Other tools

Saws very occasionally need re-sharpening. This is a job for an expert. Most tool shops will run, or be able to give information about, a saw sharpening service.

Sharpening a plane blade on an oilstone

Removing a 'burr' when sharpening a plane blade

Hammer faces (or peins) must be kept clean and polished by rubbing on smooth sandpaper when necessary. Try squares are precision tools which must not be knocked or dropped.

Woodwork benches

A great deal of woodworking can be carried out on a table, or even on a sawing trestle. Some form of temporary vice attached to the table will be an advantage because it

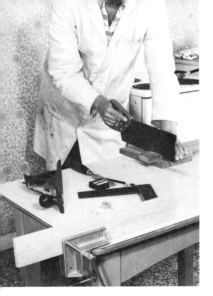

Woodworking on the kitchen table

A home-made woodwork bench

enables pieces of wood being worked to be held firmly. The possession of a bench specially made for woodworking is, however, a great advantage. A number of firms sell woodwork benches, some specialising in making them for the home woodworker. One of simple construction is described here. The making of this bench is well within the capabilities of an inexperienced woodworking enthusiast. Although made on simple lines, the construction is strong and robust and the bench will stand up to many years of hard wear. Many different types of vice are made for fitting to such a bench. That shown in the photograph on page 6 is fitted with a Record 52D vice.

If you are making your own bench it is as well to make it to suit your own requirements of height, length and width. The bench described here is 1050 mm long by 450 mm wide and stands 800 mm high. Other heights may be more suitable for a tall or for a short person. The length or width of the bench top can be increased if required. The following is a list of materials necessary for making the bench shown:

4 legs	778 mm by 45 mm by 45 mm
1 top	1050 mm by 450 mm by 22 mm
	(probably two or three pieces
	to make this width)
2 rails	1050 mm by 200 mm by 22 mm
2 rails	400 mm by 150 mm by 22 mm
2 rails	790 mm by 75 mm by 22 mm
2 rails	310 mm by 75 mm by 22 mm
2 top	
fixing strips	700 mm by 22 mm square
2 top	
fixing strips	220 mm by 22 mm square
1 bench stop	150 mm by 35 mm by 30 mm

Glue; 50 mm gauge 10 screws; 40 mm gauge 8 screws; 75 mm by 10 mm coach bolt; washer; wing nut.

The dimensions given are the finished sizes and make no allowance for waste.

All parts are glued and screwed together and an adjustable bench stop for planing is incorporated. Any wood is suitable, although a hardwood will wear better. The bench shown here was made from an African wood called Meranti. When making this type of framework, check at every stage that each frame is exactly 'square'. A coat of polyurethane clear varnish applied with a brush will provide a good finish to the bench.

fig 29: making the bench (stage 1) back and front frames

fig 30: making the bench (stage 2) end rails joined to front and back frames

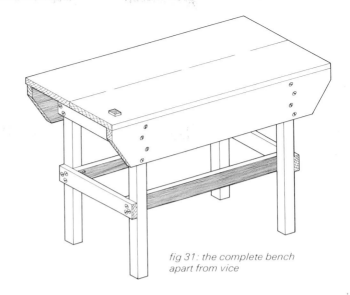

fig 31: the complete bench apart from vice

Bench equipment

Whether you possess a woodwork bench or not, there are three items which can be useful additions to your growing list of equipment. These three items can either be made or purchased. All three are of simple construction and their sizes depend upon the choice of the person making them. The first is a sawing stool or sawing trestle (sawing horse is another name). Sawing stools are used in pairs to enable

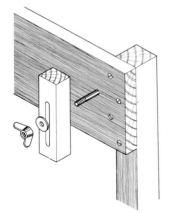

fig 32: method of fitting planing stop to bench

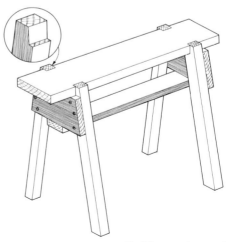

fig 33: a sawing trestle

long or large boards to be positioned for sawing, marking or other working. They should be made from a hardwood to resist wear. Even if they are not considered necessary for sawing, these stools are well worth acquiring. You can easily carry them to jobs elsewhere in a house or garden and they make good, although small, work benches. The addition of a temporary vice increases the amount of work for which they are suitable. They are also of value for standing on to reach high places when painting or decorating or for sitting on when you feel tired, or when carrying out work such as marking out.

The second item is a sawing board (or bench hook).

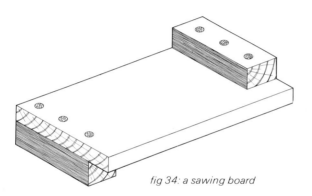

fig 34: a sawing board

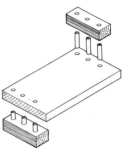

fig 35: construction of a sawing board

Sawing wood held in a sawing board

Again these are best made from a hardwood or from thick plywood. They can easily be made at home. Wood can be held quite firmly by hand in a sawing board, which is itself placed against the edge of a bench or table. Sawing boards can also be used as chiselling boards. When chiselling downwards place the work being chiselled on to the board then the bench or table top is not damaged by the sharp chisel edge. When making a sawing board, there is a temptation to screw its parts together. It is far better to joint the parts with dowels and glue. After a sawing board has been in service for some time, its surfaces become damaged by saw cuts. Eventually these will expose the ends of the screws. A saw passing over an exposed screw will quickly become blunted.

A home-made 'shooting board

The third item which you can either make or purchase is a shooting board. This is a more difficult piece of equipment

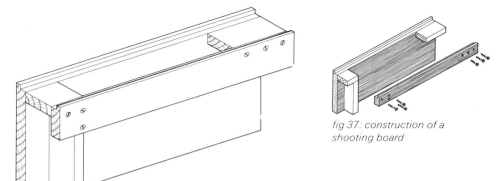

fig 37: construction of a
shooting board

fig 36: a shooting board

to make and should perhaps be left until you are more skilful. The purpose of a shooting board is to enable pieces of wood to be held firmly while their ends are 'shot' or planed. When planing the ends of wood, splits will occur at the end of the planing cuts. If the wood is placed in a shooting board this splitting does not take place. End grain can be planed without splitting by taking one of the precautions shown in the drawings. The possession of a shooting board, however, makes the task easier and quicker.

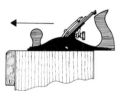

fig 38: planing end grain by
chamfering end

fig 39: planing end grain
protected by spare wood

One last item of equipment which should be mentioned before closing this chapter is a G-cramp. G, or similar cramps, are invaluable for holding wood firmly to a bench or table when it is being worked or for holding parts together when they are being jointed with glue or screws.

3 Constructions for woodworking

Despite the increased use of metals, plastics and other materials in the manufacture of many articles which were at one time made from wood, there is more wood used today than at any time in history. Those who have worked in a variety of materials will know why this is so. Wood is the most versatile and easily worked of the constructional materials. What is more it can be worked with the minimum of tools and special equipment. Very large structures can be built from wood without special machinery. On the other hand wood cannot be easily bent, cast, pressed or moulded as can the other solid materials. It also possesses certain weaknesses such as easy splitting along the grain. Because of these qualities and defects, special methods of construction have been developed for the making of wooden articles and structures. Some of these methods have been practised for hundreds of years, others are very recent, modern introductions. Methods of construction suitable for the home woodworking enthusiast are described in this chapter.

Nailing

The most common method of construction is by nailing. Nails can be purchased by weight at so many pence per kilogramme, half kilogramme or quarter kilogramme. You will also be able to purchase them in small pre-packed quantities. Purchasing by weight is cheaper than buying packeted nails, but only if you use all the nails you buy. For heavy work such as flooring, roof joists, fencing and the making of large boxes, the common wire (French) nail is available in lengths from 25 mm to 150 mm. The oval nail (or oval brad) is of more value to the home woodworker. Made in lengths from 12 mm to 75 mm, their small heads and oval section minimise splitting as the nails are driven into wood. Always place the oval with the grain. Lost head nails are a more modern nail for purposes similar to those

fig 40: types of nail (1) wire nail (2) oval nail (3) lost head nail (4) panel pin (5) hardboard pin

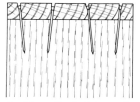

fig 41: method of dovetail nailing

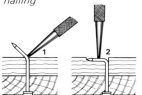

fig 42: clinching a nail (stages 1 and 2)

fig 43: clinching a nail (stage 3)

fig 44: nailed frame joint, staggered nails

fig 45: nailing a box bottom, nails some distance from corners

for which wire nails are made. Panel pins are of particular value. Their thin pins and small heads make them suitable for much of the light nailing carried out by home woodworkers. Lengths from 10 mm to 50 mm. Hardboard pins – usually 20 mm long – are hardened nails for pinning hardboard to frames. The tough pin can be hammered through the hard surface of the board without the pin buckling.

Rules when nailing

Rust, dirt, grease or glue spots on the face of a hammer head will cause nails to bend as they are driven home. You

'Dovetail' nailing

Punching nail heads below the wood surface

should clean the face on sandpaper. Dovetail nailing is considerably stronger than straight nailing and should be practised where possible. Nails should be clinched (see diagrams) when making nailed frames. If nails are placed in line along the grain, the wood will split as they are hammered home. So, stagger the nails. Several sizes of nail punch for 'punching' nail heads below the wood surface make a useful addition to a tool kit. The punch holes can be filled in with putty, wood filler, wood stopper or Polyfilla if you wish.

Screwing

Screwed constructions in wood are very strong and have the advantage that, unless they are also glued, they can be taken to pieces merely by withdrawing the screws. Many articles can be made just by screwing, using no other form of construction. Wood screws are sold in a vast range of different types and different sizes and are made from various materials. The most frequently used sizes are sold in boxes of 200, others in boxes of 100 and some in boxes containing fifty screws. More often they are purchased in tens, sold loose over the counter, but then they tend to be more expensive per screw than when they are bought by the box. The most common material from which woodscrews are made is steel, but brass, copper and aluminium screws are also available as well as screws coated with black enamel, copper, zinc, cadmium and chromium.

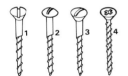

fig 46: types of wood screw (1) countersunk screw (2) round head screw (3) raised head screw (4) Pozidriv screw

The three types of woodscrews you are most likely to find to be of value are countersunk screws; the round-head and raised-head screws are also occasionally needed. Pozidriv screws are a modern screw of fairly recent introduction. Note that Pozidriv screws are screwed with a twin, or double-start thread along their whole length and that the heads require the use of a special Phillips or a Pozidriv screwdriver. Most work requires countersunk screws. Many fittings are screwed to wood with round-head or with raised-head screws. Screws are sold by length. Note this is the effective length as shown in the drawing. Another dimension of measurement is the gauge or diameter of a woodscrew. The most frequently used gauge diameters are gauges 4, 6, 8 and 10. Note there is no relationship with millimetres in this gauge size. Gauge diameters from as thin as 0 to as fat as 50 are available.

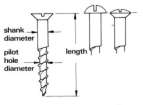

fig 47: measurements of wood screws

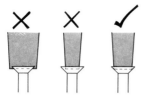

fig 48: width of screwdriver
blade

fig 49: method of sharpening
end of screwdriver

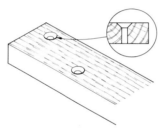

fig 50: first stage of screwed
frame joint

Some rules when screwing

Always drill correct size holes to receive any particular
woodscrew. If you do not do so either the wood will split or
the screw will fail to hold securely. This normally means
three separate drillings. First the shank hole, then the pilot
hole for the thread part and finally, if necessary, the
countersinking of the shank hole. Drill sizes for the common
gauges are:

Gauge	4	6	8	10
Shank drill diameter	3 mm	4 mm	5 mm	6 mm
Pilot drill diameter	2 mm	2 mm	3 mm	4 mm

Try to use the correct width of screwdriver blade. Too
wide or too narrow a blade will result in damaged wood or
damaged screw slots. Avoid damaging the screw slot. Such
damage is not only unsightly, but the slivers of metal which
result from the damage can injure your fingers and damaged
screws are very difficult to remove. Stagger screws along
the grain to minimise splitting and to spread the pressure
area of the screws. About two-thirds of the length of a
wood screw should be in the lower part of a screwed joint.
Screwed joints which are also glued are probably the
strongest of all wood joints because no part of the wood
comprising the joints needs to be removed. The method of
making a screwed frame joint is shown in the drawings. A
screwed corner joint is also shown.

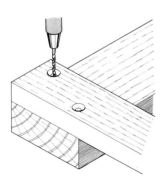

fig 51: second stage of
screwed frame joint, boring
pilot hole

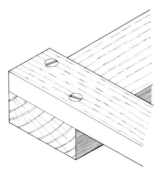

fig 52: assembled screwed
frame joint

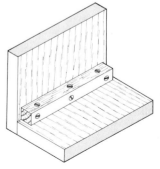

fig 53: screwed corner joint
for chipboard

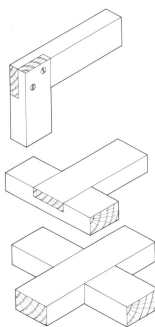

Halving joints

You can make many strong-framed constructions with halving joints, so named because half of the wood from each of the two parts of the joint is removed by sawing or chiselling. There are three common types: corner halving, Tee halving and cross halving. Corner halvings often need to be screwed or nailed in addition to being glued. Tee and cross halvings normally only need to be glued. The processes involved in making these joints are shown in the drawings. All three halvings are made either by sawing half of the wood from an end or by sawing and chiselling grooves. When sawing, the saw 'kerf' must be made to the 'waste' side of the line of the joint. Failure to 'saw into the waste' will result in loose joints. When chiselling a halving groove, chisel from both sides of the wood in turn to prevent splitting the back of the groove as the chisel passes across for its final cut.

fig 54: three types of halving joint; corner, tee and cross halvings

Method of sawing a halving joint

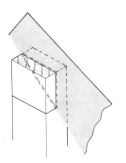

fig 55: first stage of sawing
halving

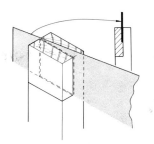

fig 56: second stage of sawing halving and 'sawing into
waste'

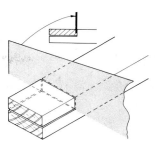

fig 57: third stage of sawing
halving and 'sawing into
waste'

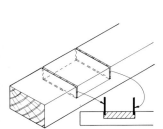

fig 58: first stage of sawing
halving groove and 'sawing
into waste

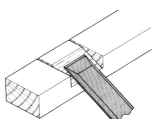

fig 59: second stage of
cutting halving groove

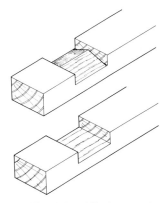

fig 60: third and final stage of
cutting halving groove

Rebated corner joint

One of the most effective methods for joining box corners is
by rebated corner joints. The rebate is the cut-away portion
of one of the pieces being joined. The method of making a
rebated corner is shown in figs 61 and 62. This joint can be
glued and not nailed, but it is preferable both to glue and
nail. You must be careful where you place the nails. They
will tend to be very near to the end of the wood and may
split the end when hammered home. Dovetail nailing of a
rebated corner will increase its strength.

*Opposite: the assembled joint
using 'knock-down' con-
struction*

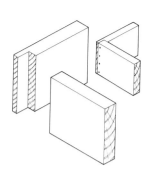

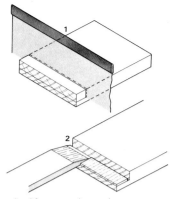

fig 61: a rebated corner joint

fig 62: stages in cutting a rebate

Housing joints

If you require to join a shelf to an upright or to a partition, or wish to join partitions to box sides, one of the strongest of jointing methods is by housing one part into the other. Two types of housing joints are shown in the drawings. These are the through housing, so called because the groove is cut from one edge of the wood through to the other, and the stopped housing in which the groove stops short of one

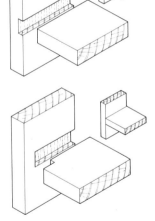

fig 63: through and stopped housing joints

Chopping the recess for a stopped housing joint. Notice the wood being worked is protected from the G-cramp by a piece of spare wood

fig 64: stages in cutting a housing groove

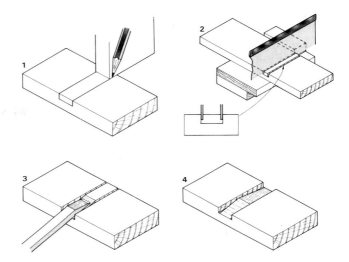

fig 65: stages in cutting a stopped housing

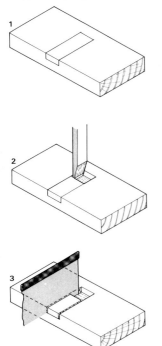

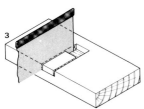

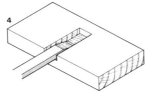

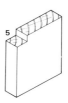

edge. The processes involved in making both of these housings are shown in a series of drawings. If you wish to make successful, strong housing joints, the groove must be exactly the same in width as the thickness of the piece of wood which is to fit into the groove. To make sure of this, the groove width should be marked directly from the shelf or partition it is being made to hold. You must also 'saw into the waste' when sawing the groove sides. Provided that housing joints are a good, tight fit, needing firm hand pressure to force the shelf into its groove, no nailing will be necessary. Glue only will hold the pieces together strongly and permanently. Stopped housings are more difficult to make than are through housings. This is because they require the chopping of a recess into which the saw can be worked when sawing the groove sides. Stopped housings have, however, the advantage that the jointing method cannot be seen from one edge.

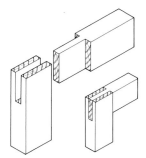

fig 66: the two parts of a
bridle joint

fig 67: the stages in making a
bridle joint

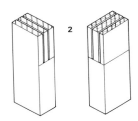

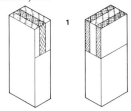

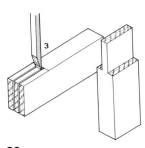

Bridle joints

A very strong corner frame joint is the bridle, an example of
which is given in the drawing. When making a corner bridle
joint, the marking out of both parts is identical. The sawing
of each part however is different. One half of the joint is
sawn so that the saw cuts are outside the lines, the second
half with the saw cuts inside the lines. The waste from the
part sawn inside the line is chopped out with a chisel and
mallet. The shoulders of the other piece are sawn. When
sawing down the grain of a bridle joint adopt the same
method as was shown for the sawing of halvings.

A well-made bridle joint

Mortise and tenon joints

One of the most common of all woodworking constructions
is the mortise and tenon joint. If you look around you will
find many examples of this constructional method – in your
house, in furniture and in the construction of buildings.
Only two types are shown here, but there must be hundreds
of different types of this form of joint. It is used in making
door and table frames; for joining rails in chests or in
wardrobes; for joining ceiling and roof joists in first-class
building practice; and for countless other constructional
uses. The hole is called a mortise, sometimes spelt mortice.
The tenon is the projecting piece which fits into the mortise.
They must fit together accurately for the join to be
successful. Some practice is required before you can make
good mortises and tenons, but persevere and you will
succeed. The tenon is sawn by using the same processes by
which halvings are cut. The processes involved in chopping

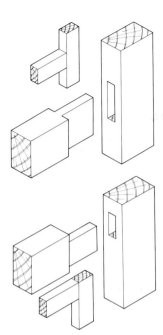

fig 68: two mortise and tenon joints

fig 69: stages in chopping a mortise

Chopping a mortise

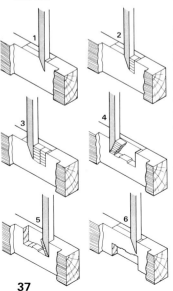

a mortise are shown in six drawings. The tool for chopping a mortise should preferably be a mortise chisel, although other chisels can be used if necessary. A mallet is needed for driving the chisel into the wood. If a mortise is to be cut right through the wood from edge to edge, holes are chopped from both edges and the two holes meet in the middle. Some mortises are 'stopped'. Their depth is a half or two-thirds of the depth of the wood into which they are cut. When chopping a stopped mortise, its depth must be measured by inserting a ruler or a marked strip of wood into the hole.

'Knock-down' jointing

You may wish to use 'knock-down' or K.D. methods of construction. Many different types of K.D. jointing fittings are manufactured. A few of the more easily available are shown here. The value of these modern jointing methods is that they allow strong joints to be made quickly, easily and

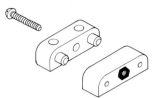

fig 70: nylon corner joint block

Nylon joint blocks screwed into a corner joint

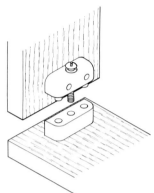

fig 71: nylon joint block screwed to a corner

accurately. Added to these advantages, the parts can be speedily taken apart so that the whole construction can be 'knocked-down' to a flat packet for easy transport. K.D. joints are particularly suited to chipboard, for which they have really been designed. Three common K.D. methods are shown in drawings. The first is the popular joint block. Two nylon blocks are screwed, one against each face, to the inside of a corner. They are held together by a steel bolt which locks the two boards to each other. The second employs purpose-made nylon plugs which are glued into holes bored into the end of one part of a corner joint. Into these plugs screws are driven through holes and plastic screw caps in the second part of the joint. The caps are then snapped shut over the screw heads to cover and hide them. The third method using either Rawlplugs or nylon inserts is similar to that using nylon plugs. Screw caps can also be used with this method. Each of the three methods shown can be quickly unscrewed for 'knocking-down'.

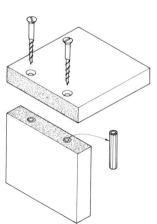

fig 73: nylon plugs instead of Rawlplugs

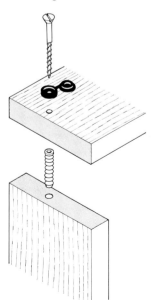

fig 72: screwed corner joint using Rawlplugs

fig 74: screwing a corner joint using nylon screw plug and polythene screw cap

Hinges

Sooner or later you will need to hang a door with hinges. Of the wide range of hinges which can be purchased today, three types are shown. These are those by which doors are most often hung. The three hinges shown are lay-on hinges, butt hinges and pivot hinges. When hanging a door you will usually need a pair of hinges. For large doors such as wardrobe doors three or even four hinges may be necessary. Lay-on hinges and butt hinges can be purchased in a variety of sizes. Choose that size most suitable for the particular door you are hanging. Pivot hinges are made only in one size suitable for hanging small, light doors up to say 600 mm high.

Lay-on hinges

These are made from steel, plated with brass, zinc, cadmium or chromium. The drawing shows only one type. Other shapes, but working on the same principle can be bought. Lay-on hinges are very easy to fit. Just lay each hinge in position on the door edge and screw it in place with two countersunk screws of the correct length and gauge for your particular size of hinge. Then hold the door against the cupboard or cabinet against which it is to be hung and screw the second flap of the hinge to the inside cupboard wall. Again make certain the screws are the correct size. When screwing to the cupboard, accurate positioning is needed if the door is to swing properly. Drive only one screw through each hinge flap into the cupboard wall and test the door swing before putting in the second screw. If the door does not swing properly you can then take out the first screws, re-position the hinges and put in the second screws. The first screw holes will have to be plugged by gluing small strips of wood in the wrong holes before replacing the screws in their correct positions.

Butt hinges

'Butts' are made from steel or from brass. Brass butts are either plate or solid. The best brass butts are solid-drawn, but they are quite expensive, although plate butt hinges are no more expensive than other types. Butts are more difficult to fit than are lay-on hinges. Each part of each hinge must be fitted into a purpose-cut recess which must be exactly the right size and position for your particular hinge. If, however, care is taken in positioning and cutting these recesses, butts are one of the best and strongest of hinges. They have been used for two centuries or more and continue to be one of the most popular of all hinges.

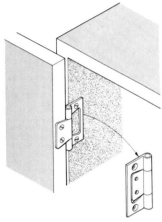

fig 75: a door hung with lay-on hinges

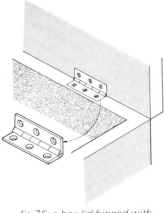

fig 76: a box lid hinged with butt hinges

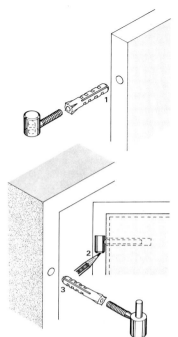

Pivot hinges

Pivot hinges may be purchased in pre-packed sets of pairs or of several pairs, complete with nylon or plastic inserts. These hinges are made from steel which has been brass plated or chromium plated. They are suitable only for hanging light doors. In fact pivot hinges were really designed for hanging small, flat doors made from chipboard. They are very easy to fit. First, holes are bored into the door edge to receive the plastic inserts. Those parts of the hinges containing pivot holes are screwed into these inserts and turned upside down. The position of the bottoms of the inverted hinges are then marked against the front cabinet edge. This gives the positions for the holes which take the inserts for the pivot part of the hinges. When these have been screwed in place, the hinge parts on the door edge are turned the right way up — with the pivot holes downwards. The door can now be hung and should straight away swing properly. With pivot hinges some adjustment is possible by screwing or unscrewing parts in or out of their inserts.

fig 77: screw-in pivot hinge for a door

Drawer construction

A simple method of constructing a drawer is shown. This method produces a strong construction. Drawers made in this way are quite strong enough for very heavy use, such as they would receive if fitted into kitchen furniture. The drawer sides are rebate jointed to the front and housing jointed to the back. The box is then glued and pinned together. The bottom, made from hardboard or plywood, is glued on to strips which have been glued and pinned inside at the bottom of the sides and to the back of the front. When making drawers remember to make quite sure that each part fits exactly into the space it is to occupy in its compartment before you start constructing. If you forget to trim each part to size first, you will find great difficulty in trying to make the drawer run smoothly in the place it has been made to fit once it has been completed.

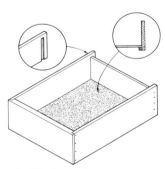

fig 78: simple drawer construction

Nailing the front joint of a drawer

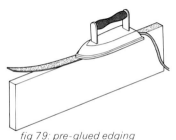

fig 79: pre-glued edging ironed to chipboard

Pre-glued edging strip

A recently introduced do-it-yourself edging strip which can be permanently glued to the edges of chipboard, thick plywood or blockboard with the aid of a domestic hot iron is shown in a drawing. This edging strip can be purchased in different wood grains — either real wood or plastic imitation wood — or in white or coloured plastics. It is backed with a plastic glue which melts under the action of the hot iron, but sets quite firmly when cold. It is used to cover the unsightly edges of chip and other manufactured boards.

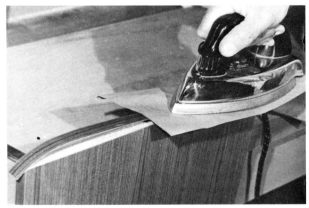

Ironing on pre-glued vinyl edging to the end of chipboard

Removing the surplus of edging strip with sandpaper

4 Wood finishes and glues

Wood finishing

Unprotected wooden surfaces are difficult to keep clean
and can easily become dirty or damaged. Stains, varnishes,
polishes, oils and paints can be applied on wood to provide
protection or decoration. These 'finishes' protect woodwork
against handling and are also easy to clean. Stains,
varnishes and polishes will enhance the grain and texture of
wood. Some finishes are water and heat resistant and are
not damaged by water, hot tea cups or hot plates. There is a
large variety of modern wood-finishing materials on sale.
These are usually quite easy to apply, but it is necessary to
follow two simple rules. First you must always read the
maker's instructions and follow them as carefully as
possible. After all the makers will know exactly how the
materials should be applied. Second, the surfaces to be
finished must be smooth, clean and free from glue spots,
oil, dirt, dust and blemishes. A good quality polish or
varnish properly applied will show up blemishes very clearly
and make them even more unsightly than they were before
the finish was applied. Time spent on the preparation of a
wooden surface by removing tool marks, scratches, hammer
marks, dents, torn grain, dirt and other blemishes is amply
repaid by the quality of the resulting surfaces after wood
finishes have been applied. Good surfaces ready for
finishing are obtained by sanding.

fig 80: tearing sandpaper
against a strip of wood

Sandpapering

Three main types of 'sandpaper' can be purchased. These
are – glasspaper, garnet paper and aluminium oxide paper.
For most purposes it doesn't really matter which you
choose. Glasspaper is cheaper than the other two types, but
doesn't last so long because it wears out more quickly, so
the few pence saved is not much of a gain. Numerous
grades of sandpapers are made. The following table shows
the grades you are most likely to require.

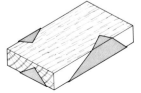

fig 81: wrapping sandpaper
around a sanding block

	fine	medium	coarse
Glasspaper grade	1	$1\frac{1}{2}$	M2
Garnet paper grade	3/0	2/0	$\frac{1}{2}$
Aluminium oxide paper	120	100	60

You can buy coarser or finer grades than these three if you
need them. Sandpaper can be purchased in sheets each
measuring about 280 mm by 230 mm which can be cut into
six convenient size pieces for sanding purposes. This can be
done by tearing against a strip of wood. Small packets of
sandpaper cut ready to size for immediate use can be
purchased in many shops.

When sanding a surface wrap the piece of sandpaper
around a block of wood. This not only helps to keep the
surface you are sanding truly flat, but also prevents the
sandpaper from wearing out quickly. An old saying that
'sandpaper is the most expensive tool in a workshop' rings
even more true if it is wasted by adopting careless methods
of working.

Sanding wood

To obtain a good surface ready for the application of any
wood finish first plane the wood to as smooth a surface as
possible. Then wrap a piece of coarse sandpaper — say M2
glasspaper — around a block of wood and, pressing firmly
downwards with the hands, work the sandpaper all over the
surface *always following the direction of the grain*. When
all defects have been removed repeat the operation but with
a finer grade — say Grade 1 glasspaper. If you sand across
the grain, the resulting scratches are very difficult to
remove. Sand with the grain and the scratches will not
show. This sanding in two stages should produce a smooth
clean surface ready for any finish. If this takes longer than
you expected, remember this time has been well spent if
you wish to see a first-rate finish on your woodwork.

*Sandpaper wrapped around a
cork block*

Wood finishes

The more common wood finishes are: stains, french polishes, polyurethane varnishes, polyester varnishes, cellulose lacquers, oils, wax polishes, paints, creosote. Some of these are not suitable for the less experienced woodworker. Only those which can be applied without difficulty are described.

Stains

You may find some of your work needs staining when you wish to match the colour of some existing woodwork. However I would advise avoiding staining if possible. Most woodwork looks best with a 'natural' finish which allows the original colours in the wood to be seen to full advantage. If staining is necessary it is probably best to buy ready-made, oil-based stains which can be purchased in cans of convenient sizes ready for immediate application. These can be applied with a brush or with clean rags. After staining, a polish or other finish will be necessary.

French polish

French polishes are shellacs dissolved in methylated spirit with the addition of hardening gums. Some modern french polishes are thin polyurethane lacquers. To achieve a full french polish is a process beyond the skills of all but the expert, but french polish is a very good wood sealer for the less experienced. A pleasing soft sheen can be obtained by applying two coats of white french polish with a brush, allowing them to dry, then lightly sanding to a very smooth surface with grade 0 glasspaper. This seals the wood which can then be polished with a wax polish.

Polyurethane varnishes

Clear polyurethane varnish applied in two brush coats with drying intervals between produces an excellent finish. If the second coat is allowed to harden thoroughly for six or seven days and then lightly rubbed along the grain with fine wire wool, the resulting sheen is very pleasing. Polyurethane finishes are sufficiently heat proof to resist boiling water without damage. Tinted polyurethane varnishes produce pleasing coloured finishes through which the wood grain can be seen.

Oils

Teak oil, which is on sale in many shops, is an excellent finish for all dark-coloured woods. Applied with a soft rag in two coats with an interval of a day or so between. The resulting oiled surface is matt and smooth with a dull sheen which suits dark coloured woods. Linseed oil can be rubbed into wood to give an oiled finish but drying takes several weeks. Thin coats of linseed oil rubbed on hardwoods at weekly intervals over a period of several months produces a pleasing golden hard-wearing sheen.

Wax polishes

Floor and furniture wax polishes provide excellent, easily applied finishes. A sealer is necessary to prevent the wax sinking into the wood. French polish; thin, clear cellulose lacquer; polyurethane varnish thinned with white spirit; are good sealers for this purpose. The wax is applied and polished with clean rags or dusters.

Paints

Softwoods such as pines and red deal can be painted without difficulty – either a primer coat followed by an undercoat followed by a top (gloss) coat or two coats of polyurethane paint. Hardwood surfaces, however, must be 'filled in' before they can be painted. Such filling can consist of a thin paste of Polyfilla or plaster of Paris rubbed in with coarse rag and sanded when quite dry.

fig 82: brush suitable for applying any type of wood finish

Creosote

Two brush coats of creosote will protect fencing, sheds, gate-posts and other outdoor woodwork against rotting. Further brush coats every second year are advisable.

Cleaning brushes

Brushes must be cleaned after use. The fluid most often used is white spirit (turps substitute) although methylated spirit must be used for cleaning brushes which have applied french polish. After cleaning in these liquids, brushes should be washed with hot water and soap. In between coats, brushes can be suspended in a tin or bottle of white spirit.

Glues

If you read and obey the instructions printed on the containers in which they are purchased, modern glues are strong and reliable. They can be purchased from many shops in cans, tubes, plastic containers or packets in small or large quantities as and when you need them. The three glues of most value to woodworkers are pva, urea-formaldehyde and impact glue.

fig 83: brush soaking in white spirit between coats

fig 84: PVA glue from a
squeegee plastic container

Polyvinyl acetate (pva) glues are the easiest of all modern glues to use. They can be purchased in ready-to-use plastic squeegee containers which can be thrown away when empty. The glue is squeezed directly on to the surfaces to be glued. The white liquid glue sets chemically in about three or four hours depending on room temperature. On warm days the glue sets more quickly than on cold days. Pva glue is sufficiently strong for all woodwork, but as it is not waterproof, it is unsuitable for woodwork which might get damp. Joints made with pva glues need cramping or holding together tightly until the glue sets. Examples are Borden wood glue, Evostik wood glue, Croid polystik.

Urea-formaldehyde glues make strong and practically waterproof joints in woodwork. They are suitable for woodwork which might be exposed to damp situations. Two types can be purchased. The first is a white powder (e.g., Cascamite) which must be mixed with water to form a thick syrup before it can be applied. The second type is purchased in a two-part pack. One part is a thick syrup, the second a thin liquid hardener (e.g., Aerolite). Joints made with these glues must be kept under pressure while setting takes place. Setting is a chemical reaction which is quicker (about two hours) in warmer conditions than in colder.

Impact glues are rubber bases in solvents. They allow surfaces to hold directly they are placed together, that is on impact. They are used for gluing plastic laminates (e.g., Formica) to wood, or for gluing fabrics to wood, but they are not sufficiently strong for wood to wood joins. The thick paste-like glue is thinly spread over surfaces to be joined and then you wait for about fifteen minutes to allow the glue to become tacky. The surfaces are then placed against each other and are instantly held together. Examples are Evostik, Bostik.

Three other glues you may come across are Scotch glue, epoxy resin glue and hot melt glue.

Scotch glues are made from animal bones and hides. They can be purchased ready-to-use (e.g., Croid aero glue) or can be made from 'pearl' glue — small pieces of solid glue which need to be mixed with water and then heated to a liquid state. These are cheap, very strong, but not waterproof, nor easy to use.

The most common *epoxy resin glue* is Araldite. Sold in two-part packs of two tubes each containing a thick resin. The two resins must be mixed prior to use. Not suitable for woodwork because they are very expensive, epoxy resins will join together any two materials — china, earthenware, glass, metals, most plastics. They are of value for those odd jobs that occur which involve these other materials when woodworking.

Hot melt glues
These are mentioned because iron-on edging veneer strips are coated with hot-melt glue on their back surfaces. They are plastics which melt when heated and set firmly when cold. They cannot be purchased as glues from shops as can the other glues described.

Cramping
When pieces of wood are glued to each other they usually need to be held tightly together until the glue sets. Parts can often be held together with nails or screws while glue sets, but some form of cramping is sometimes needed. A bench vice makes a good cramping device for some work. A pile of

fig 85: sash cramps used for holding frame while glue sets

Cramping glued work with G-cramps

A glued bridle joint cramped with a G-cramp

Cramping a small table frame with sash (bar) cramps

books will often be sufficiently heavy to hold some joints — but place newspaper between the top piece of wood and the bottom book. G-cramps are a valuable addition to your tool kit and, if you can afford to buy a sash cramp or two, the range of work which you can glue together is greatly increased.

5 Woodwork design

Before you start making anything from wood think out its design. I can think of nothing more disappointing when woodworking than to spend a great deal of time, energy and money in making a piece of work only to find that the result looks wrong or is not going to work properly. If you are copying other work or working to drawings from books or magazines then you do not need to bother much about the design. It has been worked out for you. If, however, you are starting from scratch to make something in wood, then some advice on designing is necessary. Woodwork designing is complex and many large volumes have been written on the subject. In the next few pages only the bare outlines of some of the problems involved when designing are given.

Copying existing work
If you are copying another piece of woodwork or working to printed drawings you may find that a millimetre or so added here or subtracted there, a slight change of curve, the use of different woods or finishes and other such small changes, can improve a design to your satisfaction. So, even if you like the design, there's nothing wrong in altering it to please yourself. This is one of the advantages in being able to make your own woodwork — you can please yourself.

Sketching
A good rule is always to make a sketch on paper of the piece of work you wish to make. The roughest of sketches with necessary dimensions is better than nothing. You may surprise yourself by how well you can produce a drawing once the plunge has been taken. Always put your ideas down on paper before commencing work. Paper is much, much cheaper than wood. If you make a bad drawing, or your ideas will not work out at once on paper, the drawing can easily be rubbed out and started again. Once you have

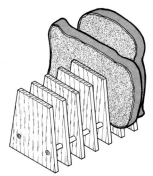

fig 86: the dimensions of a toast rack depend on the sizes of the toast

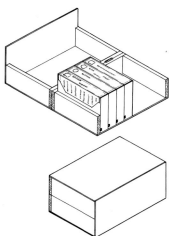

fig 87: the dimensions of a tape cassette box depend upon the number of cassettes to be housed.

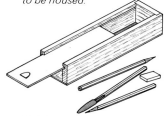

fig 88: pencils, pens, rubbers etc. must all fit inside a pencil-box

cut a piece of wood to shape, it cannot be made longer if you suddenly discover it is too short. Its shape should have been planned before it was cut.

Sizes and dimensions

The first most important element when designing is to get the sizes right. Take the examples shown in the drawings. It's no good making a toast rack until you have measured the sizes of each of the slices of toast and decided on how many slices you wish the rack to hold. There is no value in a cassette case into which cassettes will not fit because you haven't measured a cassette and decided how many cassettes the case is to hold. A pencil-box which has been made so short that your longest pencil will not fit in is going to be a constant irritation. So measure the lengths of the pens and pencils the box is to hold. A box to hold shoe-cleaning materials becomes so much firewood if it cannot contain the brushes, tins of polish and polishing dusters you need to store in it. The dimensions for a bedside wall fitting need careful planning. What do you wish to place on its shelves? Clock, books, a cup of tea. Anything else? Measure each and every item before you finally decide on the sizes of the fitting. The first rule when designing is to measure, check your measurements and then check again. Write them down on paper. Don't forget the extras which can increase the overall sizes. It is not just six pieces of toast in length. It is six pieces of toast plus seven wood thicknesses plus a few millimetres extra for ease of putting toast in and taking it out of the rack.

fig 89: a bedside shelf made to hold paperbacks, a clock and a cup and saucer

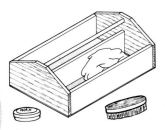

fig 90: a box for shoe-cleaning materials must be of a size to hold them

Opposite: wood abstract – cherry with bark left on. See page 62

Wood thicknesses

Having decided on the overall dimensions for a design, now give consideration to the thicknesses of each piece in the design. Wood is a strong and tough material and over-heavy parts tend to look wrong. It is better to avoid using wood which is too thick for the job in hand. Some examples are: 6 mm thick wood for the partitions of the toast rack with 9 mm diameter dowels between the partitions; wood of 6 mm or 8 mm thickness is suitable for the cassette case; the shoe-cleaning box could have sides and ends made from 10 mm or 12 mm thick wood and the bedside fitting might stand 15 mm thick shelves, although 12 mm might be more suitable. Look at these wood thicknesses in relation to the work you are doing at the time.

Human figure sizes

'Ergonomics' is the name given to the study of design as related to the human body. Many larger pieces of woodwork must be designed around the dimensions of the human figure. Some examples of the need for this are given in drawings. Of course Mr and Mrs 'Average' do not exist, but average height and reach should be taken into consideration when designing chairs, tables, stools, fitted cupboards, wardrobes and the like. The chair which is too small or too narrow, the wardrobe which is too shallow from front to back, the table which is too low, and other badly designed pieces of furniture are fairly common. There is really no need for them — remember the rule — measure, check the measurement, then measure again.

Proportions

If the overall dimensions of a design have been chosen with a view that the job is suitable for the purpose for which it has been made, then the overall proportions of the design are usually good. In other words, it will look right. Some adjustment to overall proportions may be possible. As an example, if you are making a small table you may not wish to increase its height, but you might well be able to increase its length or width to achieve what you consider to be good overall proportions.

The proportions of the various parts of a design play a most important part in the appearance of an article. Of the three tables shown in the drawings on page 53, one contains parts with proportions about right, the second with legs and rails too thin, the third with its parts too heavy. It is interesting to note that if the too thin table were made in metal, it would probably look well. This is because

fig 91: the height and reach of the 'average man'

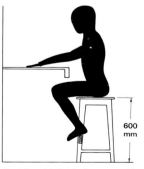

fig 92: a high kitchen stool for use at fixed work top

fig 93: kitchen cupboards must be of heights based on average women, the topmost shelf must here be reached by standing on a stool

we expect metal parts to be thinner than wooden parts because, at the back of our minds, we know that metal is stronger than wood. Certainly the use of very heavy legs and rails as shown in the third example must be avoided. It is better to aim at elegance rather than at heaviness.

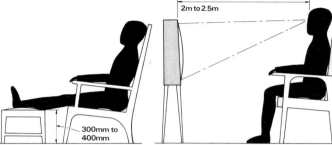

fig 94: the stool is related to the dimensions of man and chair

fig 95: good viewing distance

fig 96: proportions good

fig 97: proportions distorted by thin legs and rails

Construction

The methods by which a piece of woodwork is to be constructed are essential features of its design. There is no value at all in designing an article which cannot be constructed. Some of the elementary methods of constructing in wood are shown in the chapter on constructions. It is surprising that, even using only these simple methods, a very wide range of designs is possible. One detail requiring particular attention when constructing is the need for a constant check to ensure that parts are square, or at 90 degrees to each other. The need for squareness starts right at the beginning of any job. Each piece of wood must be square edge to side and end to length. Each join must be square and finally each part within a construction must be square. Any slight deviation from squareness shows up badly in the completed work.

Finish

The finish applied — varnish, polish, paint, etc. is an essential design feature. The choice of finish requires as much care and attention as does any other feature in the design.

fig 98: proportions distorted by thick legs and rails

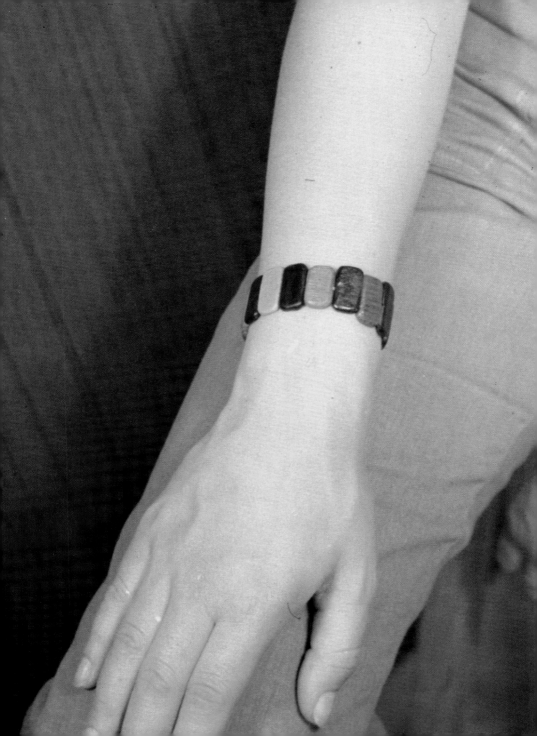

6 Examples of wood shaping

Shaping wood
There are several types of saw designed for cutting shapes from wood. You will find the most useful of these is a coping saw. Surform tools and sandpaper will smooth out roughness left by coping saw cuts. Some examples of simple-shaped work in wood are described to show you the methods of working involved.

fig 99: frying-pan spatula

A frying-pan spatula
A drawing of the spatula is shown. Thin wood (about 6 mm thick) is needed. The wood must be hard if the spatula is to be suitable for its purpose. Beech is the best wood if you can obtain it.

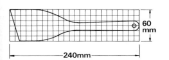

fig 100: shape of spatula on 10 mm square grid

Marking the shape on to the wood
An easy method of transferring a shape on to wood is to mark out a grid in pencil on a piece of paper and then copy the shape by transferring points from a drawing to the grid. The points are joined up to complete the curves of the shape. The paper can then be glued or pasted to the wood surface. Wait until the glue or paste has set before

Right: frying-pan spatula made from beech

Left: bangle — beech, ebony, sycamore, mahogany held together with elastic

attempting to saw the curves. When the wood has been shaped the paper grid can be sanded off with coarse sandpaper.

Making the spatula

Saw out the shape with a coping saw. Work one or two millimetres outside the line of the curves to allow for finishing to the line with a Surform tool and sandpaper. The business end of the spatula should be tapered to a sharpened edge to allow easy lifting of food from a frying-pan. Round off all the edges with sandpaper to make the spatula comfortable to handle. Sand off the paper pattern with coarse sandpaper wrapped around a block of wood. Work all over the spatula with fine sandpaper to obtain a smooth finish.

fig 101: cheese board with inlaid tile

A cheese board

This can be made from two pieces of 4 mm thick plywood glued to each other with a ceramic tile glued inside a hole cut into the upper piece of plywood. The tile's surface is

Cutting a hole for a tile – a different method

easy to clean and is also decorative. Tiles can be purchased in two sizes – approximately 110 mm square and 152 mm square. A 152 mm square tile is required for this cheese board. Tiles are usually between about 4 mm and 6 mm thick depending on their quality. Plain white or plain coloured tiles are sold. Others can be purchased which have decorative patterns or pictures glazed into their surfaces.

56

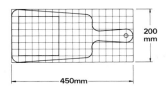

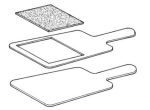

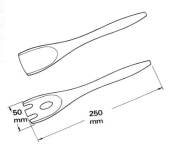

fig 102: shape of cheese
board on 25 mm square grid

fig 103: the three parts of the
cheese board

fig 104: method of sawing
square hole for tile

fig 105: salad servers from
15 mm thick wood

Decorative tiles are more expensive than plain ones, but if a suitably patterned one can be purchased, the cheese board will be a much more pleasing piece of work.

Stage 1. Copy the outline of the board on to paper with a grid of 25 mm squares. The square outline of the tile hole can be ignored for the time being. Paste or glue the paper to the upper piece of plywood.

Stage 2. The two pieces of plywood necessary for the board can be held together in a vice while their shape is cut with a coping saw and finished with sandpaper. They can be shaped separately if you wish. When the outline of the board has been worked, place the tile on to the upper piece of plywood and mark around its outline in pencil. The square of the hole is cut in two stages. First — bore 6 mm holes inside each corner of the square hole, then thread the blade of a coping saw through one of the holes and saw out the square. Saw into the squared corners from both directions to obtain sharp angles. Some adjustment to the sides of the hole may be needed by sanding to make the tile fit snugly. Glue the two pieces of shaped plywood together. A waterproof glue such as Cascamite 'One-Shot' should be used because the cheese board may need to go in with the washing-up. Place the glued pieces under a weight of some kind — a pile of books, or some tools or any other heavy object to hold the two parts together until the glue sets. When the glue has set, the shaped outer edges can be smoothed and rounded with glasspaper. Before gluing the tile into its recess give the wood (except inside the tile hole) two brush coats of clear, or tinted, polyurethane varnish, allowing about eight hours between each coat. When the second coat has dried, glue the tile into its hole using the same waterproof glue as was used for the wooden parts.

Salad servers

Wooden salad servers such as those shown in the drawing can be made following methods similar to those for making the spatula and the cheese board. When choosing wood for making salad servers — a hardwood preferably — it must be one which does not have an unpleasant smell or taste which could contaminate food. Work the hollow of both spoon and fork with the end of a Surform tool and shape the prongs of the fork before sawing the main outlines. This will enable the pieces of wood to be easily held for this part of the work. Next saw the shape of the outlines of the two pieces before finishing with a Surform tool and sandpaper.

Cheese boards — coloured tiles set in mahogany

The sectional shape across the handles could be elliptical. Part of the waste from between the fork prongs can be removed by the drilling of holes. Careful and thorough sanding to a very smooth surface is required. Salad servers can be finished by rubbing olive oil or salad oil into their surfaces with a clean rag.

Salad serving spoons. A variety of woods were used

fig 106: some suggestions for neck pendants

fig 107: neck pendants from two or more layers glued together

fig 108: a method of making a pendant

fig 109: another method; waste glued to pendant piece

Neck pendants

Items of 'jewellery' can be made from scraps of wood — pendants, earrings, necklaces, bracelets, brooches, etc. Some suggestions for pendants are shown. These can be threaded on to a leather thong for hanging round the neck. The ideas shown do not by any means exhaust the possible variations of shape. You will need pieces of wood which have a good colour and good grain, but because the pendants are small, such pieces should be easy to obtain. Either of two methods of making these can be employed. In the first, shape the pendant at the end of a longer piece than the length you want the pendant to be. This makes the wood easy to hold while it is worked. When nearly finished saw off the holding piece and smooth the sawn end of the pendant by sanding. A second method entails gluing the wood for the pendant to another piece of wood with paper between the join. The second piece enables the pendant to be held while it is worked. When finished, insert a chisel between the two pieces and split the paper. Sand the paper from the back of the pendant. Shaping can be carried out by sawing, chiselling, Surforming and sanding. Even a sharp penknife can be used.

Items such as necklaces and bangles can be built up by joining small pieces of shaped wood with strips of leather or twine. If brooches are made from wood, purpose-made clips or pins can be glued to their backs. Use Araldite (an epoxy resin glue) for this purpose. It adheres to the metal of the pin as strongly as it does to the wood.

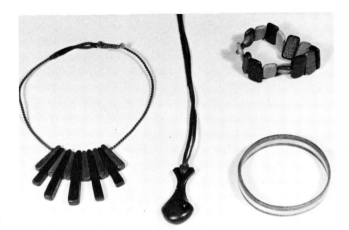

Four pieces of wooden jewel-lery

Neck pendant – ebony and ironwood

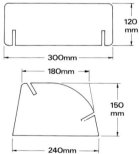

fig 110: two ends and two shelves for book rack from 9 mm plywood

fig 111: sawing into waste for grooves of book rack

Collapsible book rack

A constructional piece of woodwork requiring shaping of its parts is the book rack shown in fig 112.

To make this book rack you need:

2 plywood ends   300 mm by 120 mm by 9 mm
2 plywood shelves   180 mm by 150 mm by 9 mm

The method of shaping the rounded corners and curves is the same as was used for the items described earlier.

Method of making

(1) Saw the four rectangles to the sizes given above.

(2) Mark the grooves. A geometrical 30°, 60° set square would assist.

(3) Cut the grooves. Saw carefully into the waste of the groove sides, then cut most of the waste with a coping saw, finishing the bottoms with a chisel.

(4) Test the fit of the joints. If they are too tight they could be eased by sanding along the groove sides with sandpaper wrapped around a thin stick of wood.

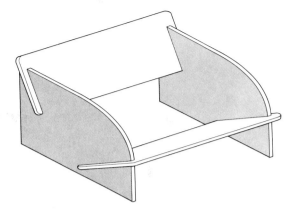

fig 112: book rack

(5) Shape the ends and the corners of the back and shelf with coping saw, Surform tool and sandpaper. Round off all corners and edges.
(6) The rack could be painted or varnished.

Kitchen spices rack
The making of the ends for this rack will give you further practice in shaping. In this example edges are shaped to a fairly complicated curve. These can be cut with a coping saw and finished with sandpaper wrapped around shaped blocks of wood. The shelves are fitted into stopped housings in the ends. The method of making these joints is described in the chapter on constructions. Strips of wood 30 mm wide and 10 mm thick are glued and pinned to the fronts of the shelves to prevent the jars of spice from falling off the rack. A suitable wood is red deal (ordinary building timber) but it needs to be of a good quality. When finished the rack's surfaces should be sanded to a very smooth finish and given two brush coats of clear polyurethane varnish. Not only will this provide a waterproof finish but it will also enhance the piney grain of the wood. The rack can be fixed to a wall with mirror plates screwed into Rawlplugs set in the wall.

To make the rack you will need the following pieces of wood. The dimensions given make no allowance for waste:

2 ends   600 mm by 100 mm by 10 mm
4 shelves   308 mm by   65 mm by 10 mm
4 edgings   300 mm by   30 mm by 10 mm

Method of making
(1) Mark the grooves on the two uprights using try square and pencil.

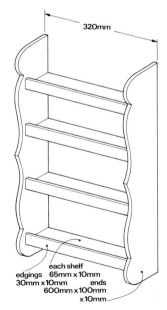

320mm

each shelf
edgings   65mm x 10mm
30mm x 10mm   ends
     600mm x 100mm
          x 10mm

fig 113: dimensions for spices rack

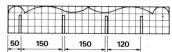

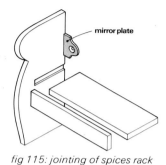

fig 114: shapes of ends and groove positions on a 25 mm grid of squares

mirror plate

fig 115: jointing of spices rack

(2) Cut the grooves — chop end recesses before sawing and chiselling.
(3) Fit shelves to the grooves — adjust grooves if necessary.
(4) Mark out, saw and sand the shapes of the ends.
(5) Clean up all inner surfaces with sandpaper.
(6) Glue shelves to ends.
(7) Glue and pin front strips to shelf edges.
(8) Clean up all outer surfaces and apply two coats of clear polyurethane varnish.

Wood sculpture

A type of wood shaping which may appeal to you is wood sculpture. This is not the same as wood carving although an interest in wood carving may arise from wood sculpting. In wood carving, the carver is attempting definite representations of shape and form. In the type of sculpture work described here, the aim is to produce abstracts in wood which give pleasure by their shape, colour, grain and form. The production of such sculptures presents no difficulties and very little experience in woodworking is necessary. You

Wood abstract — ash. See also photo on page 51

Spices rack — pine

63

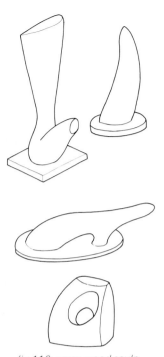

do, however, need the patience necessary to spend a lot of time in achieving a good surface finish. You also need a little artistic perception to 'see' the best forms suggested by the wood being worked. Don't be put off however. You may well surprise yourself with the beauty of the work you produce. Excellent abstracts may often be worked from grainy or knotty wood which has been thought unsuitable for construction and might even have been thrown out. Hollows, holes and curves worked on wood alter the shape and flow of grain, often with very beautiful effects.

No special tools are required. Saws, chisels and Surform tools are needed for the main shaping. A mallet is essential, and you will need bits and drills for making holes. A sharp knife is of great value, and of course plenty of sandpaper for obtaining a smooth surface. The sandpaper may need to be wrapped around strips of shaped wood to work into awkward curves and corners. A difficulty might arise as to how to hold the wood as it is worked. This problem can often be solved by leaving an extra 50 mm or so on the length for securing in a vice. This extra 50 mm is sawn off when the sculpture is nearing completion.

fig 116: some wood sculp-
tures

Wood abstract — sycamore

Right: Table place-mats and rack. See page 87. Plant stand — teak. See page 88

7 Examples of boxes

There are many methods by which wooden boxes can be made. Three of the more easy methods are shown.

The first drawing shows the most simple method of box construction. If care is taken in making sure each pair of opposite sides of the box are of equal length and their ends are sawn or planed accurately square, such boxes are easy to make and sufficiently strong for many purposes. Corner nailed 'butt' joints should always be nailed 'dovetail' fashion with the nails sloping as shown. Dovetail nailing produces much stronger corners than when nails are hammered in parallel to each other. When making a nailed box it will be stronger if you place glue between the parts, particularly between the bottom and the sides.

The second drawing shows a stronger box construction. This one is made with rebated corner joints, glued and nailed. Again, opposite sides must be of equal lengths and all ends sawn or planed accurately square.

The third drawing shows another construction. This is the strongest method of the three, but the overhanging ends may not be suitable for some boxes. The 'housing' joints — as joints involving grooves are named — can be glued together without nailing, provided you use some method of pressing the joints together while the glue sets, either cramps or a vice.

Apart from these three methods there are many other constructions for making boxes. You may like to look at boxes to examine different constructions such as 'finger' jointing, dovetailing, tongued joints and others. Such constructions are more difficult to make than the three shown here and require more skill and experience.

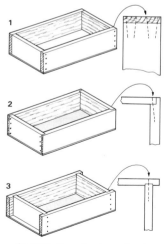

fig 117: three basic methods of making nailed boxes (1) butt joints (2) rebated corner joints (3) housing joints

Some boxes to make: a nail box

A nail box in which four different lengths or types of nails could be stored is shown. Partitioned boxes like this can be used for many purposes.

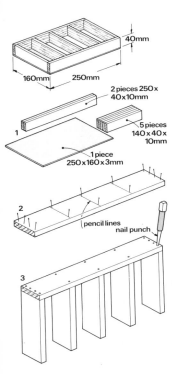

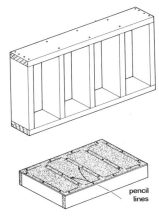

fig 118: nail box, from 10 mm thick wood, with 3 mm hardboard bottom

fig 119: nail box, assembly

Nail box

Stage 1. The box and its partitions are made from strips of wood 40 mm wide and 10 mm thick. Any softwood is suitable. After sawing the two long sides place them against each other to check they are the same length. If not, adjust them by sawing or planing. It is most important that the five 140 mm pieces are identical in length. If they are not, the box will not fit together very well. You will need the following: (no allowances have been made for waste.)

2 sides   250 mm by   40 mm by   10 mm
5 pieces   140 mm by   40 mm by   10 mm
1 bottom   250 mm by 160 mm by   3 mm

You will also need some 25 mm panel pins, some 20 mm panel pins and some glue – pva glue would be very suitable.

Stage 2. Mark squared pencil lines across the two 250 mm lengths at the partition positions and hammer 25 mm panel pins in position. Four nails are required at each corner, but only two at each partition joint.

Stage 3. Squeeze pva glue on one end of each of the five 140 mm lengths and join them to one of the 250 mm sides by hammering the panel pins in. Punch the heads of the pins just below the surface of the wood.

Stage 4. Glue and nail the second 250 mm side in place and punch the pin heads below its surface.

Stage 5. Place the frame of the box on to the rough side of the hardboard bottom and mark with a pencil all around the insides of the ends, sides and partitions. These pencil lines will act as a guide when pinning the bottom to the frame. Remember to place glue on the bottom of the frame before nailing.

Stage 6. Leave the box for at least two hours until the glue has hardened. Plane the ends and bottom level with the sides. When planing the ends, plane in towards the centre. If you plane right through, the end grain of the sides might split. Wrap a piece of sandpaper around a block of wood and sand the box to a smooth finish.

Shoe-cleaning materials box

A box with a single partition centrally along its length is shown. This box can be made for carrying shoe-cleaning materials, or cutlery, or small tools, or dusting and polishing materials from room to room around a house. The box could be made from softwood. You need the following pieces of wood for this box. The dimensions given make no allowance for waste.

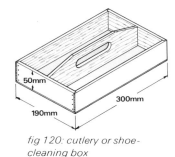

fig 120: cutlery or shoe-
cleaning box

2 sides   300 mm by 50 mm by 10 mm
2 ends   182 mm by 50 mm by 10 mm
1 partition 280 mm by 75 mm by 10 mm
1 bottom   300 mm by 190 mm by   3 mm
some 25 mm panel pins; 20 mm panel pins; glue.

Cutlery box

If you have followed the description of the making of the nail box you should be able to make this box quite easily. Differences between the making of this and the nail box are shown in drawings.

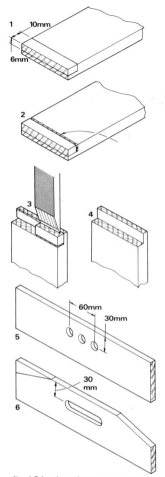

Cutting the rebates

Stage 1. Mark the rebates on both ends of the long sides with a try square, a pencil and a gauge.

Stage 2. Saw down the shoulder of the rebate. The saw cut must be made on the waste side of the squared line with the side of the saw just skimming the line.

Stage 3. Chisel the waste wood from each rebate working down the grain of the wood. Chisel back to the gauge line in several stages until the rebates are completed. The outside frame of the box can now be glued and pinned (using 25 mm pins) together.

Making the partition handle

Stage 1. Mark a line along the centre of the handle hole using a gauge set to 30 mm, or a pencil. Now bore three 25 mm diameter holes along the line.

Stage 2. Chisel the waste wood from between the holes and sandpaper the resulting handle hole to a smooth finish. Wrap the sandpaper around a piece of dowel (a round piece of wood) for this purpose.

The whole box can now be assembled and finished working in the same manner as for the nail box.

A child's trolley

This trolley is suitable for a young child who is just learning to walk. Although the making of the trolley follows some of the methods of making the nail and shoe boxes, it is a more difficult piece of work. This type of toy must be strong and tough. It is therefore best to use a hardwood. You need the following:

fig 121: showing saw cut to waste side of line (no. 4)

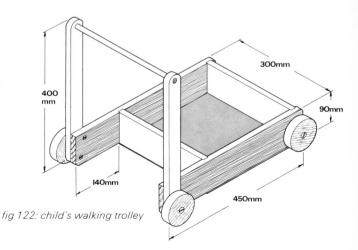

fig 122: child's walking trolley

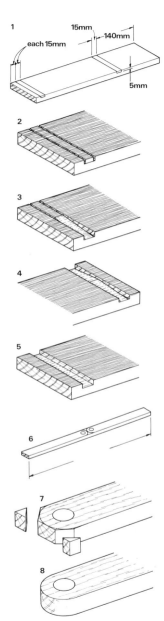

2 sides	450 mm by 90 mm by 15 mm
2 ends	280 mm by 90 mm by 15 mm
1 bottom	300 mm by 295 mm by 3 mm
2 uprights	400 mm by 40 mm by 15 mm
1 piece dowel	330 mm by 25 mm diameter
4 wheels	70 mm diameter by 25 mm

40 mm panel pins; 20 mm panel pins; four 25 mm gauge 8 steel screws; four 60 mm gauge 12 round head screws; glue. The differences between making the trolley and the other two boxes are described below.

Making the grooves

Stage 1. Mark the grooves for the joints on the inside faces of the long sides using a try square, pencil and gauge. The widths of the grooves should be exactly the same as the thickness of the ends of the short sides.

Stage 2. Working to the waste side of the lines, saw down the sides of the groove to the 5 mm gauge line.

Stage 3. Remove waste from between the saw cuts by first chiselling upwards from one end of the groove. A 10 mm or a 12 mm wide chisel would be suitable.

Stage 4. Repeat the 'uphill' chiselling from the opposite end of the groove.

Stage 5. Remove the remainder of the waste from the groove by chiselling its bottom flat.

The frame of the box can now be assembled. First clean all inside faces with sandpaper, then glue and pin the box sides together. If cramps are available it is not necessary to use pins.

The handles

Stage 1. If you can obtain a piece of wood long enough for both handles, bore the holes as shown before sawing the handles to length. If the holes are bored near the end of a strip of wood that end is liable to split open under the action of the boring tool.

Stage 2. Saw off most of the waste from the semi-circular ends.

Stage 3. Chisel and sandpaper the ends to their finished semi-circular shape.

Now glue the length of dowel into its two holes and glue and screw the handles to the box from the inside. Glue and pin the plywood bottom.

fig 123: construction of child's walking trolley (continued)

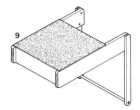

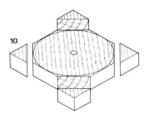

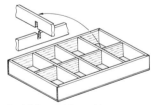

fig 124: partitioned box

Making the wheels

The wheels are made by first drawing compass circles on to pieces of hardwood, then boring a 6 mm diameter hole through the centre of each circle. The wheels are shaped by sawing waste from the corners of the squares and then chiselling and sandpapering to a circular shape. The wheels can now be screwed with the 60 mm gauge 8 screws to the trolley box. Washers between the screw heads and the wheels will save wear on the wheels.

It is advisable to paint the trolley in bright colours and stick a transfer or two over the paint. Such bright toys attract young children.

Boxes with partitions

A box in which collections of rocks, fossils, shells, coins, etc. could be stored is illustrated. No dimensions are given on the drawing because these will vary according to the contents of the box.

Halving joints are made at the places where partitions cross each other.

Above right: child's trolley ready to be painted

Right: partitioned box – pine

Wall book rack — white and
teak 'Target' vinyl-coated
chipboard. See page 81

Ornament shelving —
mahogany

Milk-bottle holder — pine and
plywood

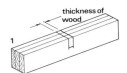

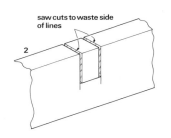

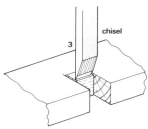

fig 125: note saw cuts to waste side of lines

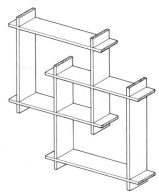

fig 126: ornaments shelving

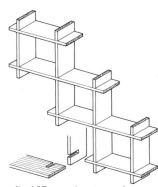

fig 127: another type of ornaments shelving

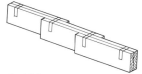

fig 128: marking out pieces for ornaments shelves

Marking halving joints

If several halving joints are to be made in line with each other, hold the pieces of wood together in the fingers, with a G-cramp or in a vice and mark all the halvings at the same time. This ensures the joints will be in a straight line to receive the long partition.

Cutting the halvings

Stage 1. Taking each marked piece in turn, carefully saw along the squared lines with one side of the saw skimming the line — sawing into the waste so that the halving grooves finish the exact thickness of the pieces which are to fit into them.

Stage 2. Chisel out the waste wood from between the saw cuts, working back to the gauge line with several cuts. Rest the wood as it is chiselled on to a scrap of waste wood. This not only prevents chisel damage to the bench or table top, but also helps to obtain a clean chisel cut on the underside of each groove.

When all the halvings have been cut, the box can be assembled using the methods already described.

Ornaments shelving

Two types of sets of shelves which can be fixed to a wall to hold ornaments are illustrated. The sizes and number of

Ornaments shelving — a wood called limba

fig 129: mirror plate for
securing shelves to wall

compartments can be varied according to the wishes of the
person making the shelves. Use hardwoods. This type of
shelving is jointed with halvings which were explained in
the description of the making of a partitioned box.

While marking the halvings the pieces should be held
together to make certain that the shelves and partitions are
in line with and square to each other.

No glue is needed between the joins if they are made to
fit tightly. The shelves are fixed to a wall by screwing a pair
of mirror plates to the back edges of the uprights and into
Rawlplugs in the wall. Mirror plates can be purchased in
many shops.

Milk-bottle holder

This milk-bottle container, which carries its own indicator
to tell the milkman how many pints are required, is of easy
construction, although it may take a long time to make. Use
a softwood and paint the completed job.

You will require the following. Finished sizes are given.
2 sides
180 mm by 175 mm by 12 mm
1 base
175 mm square by 12 mm thick
2 handle supports
180 mm by 30 mm by 12 mm
1 handle
223 mm by 12 mm dowel
2 strips for one side
199 mm by 30 mm by 10 mm
For the other side:
2 pieces plywood
199 mm by 160 mm by 3 mm
4 strips plywood
4 mm thick
1 hexagon for numeral indicator
130 mm by 130 mm by 3 mm plywood
1 short length of 6 mm dowel for pivot.
Nails, glue.

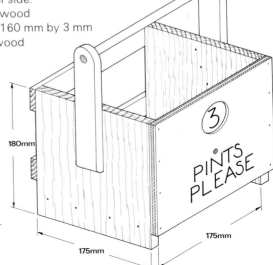

180mm

175mm

175mm

fig 130: milk-bottle holder

Method of making

Some of the processes involved have already been explained in the description of earlier pieces of work.
Stage 1. Saw and shape pieces for the handle supports. Glue and pin them to the sides with 20 mm panel pins from the insides. Punch the nail heads below the surface. Note that the grain of the sides and of the handle supports follows a vertical line.
Stage 2. Glue and nail the ends to the base with 40 mm

Dressing-table stool – white Contiplas and mahogany Contiboard. See page 79

oval nails or panel pins. Glue the dowel handle in to the supports.

Stage 3. Glue and nail the two 30 mm by 10 mm strips on one side.

Stage 4. Mark and saw out a hexagon from the 130 mm square piece of plywood.

Stage 5. Make up the indicator shown. A 6 mm dowel pivot is glued in the centre of the hexagon to fit in holes in the front and rear ply pieces. The side strips should be thicker

Blanket chest – white and mahogany Contiplas. See page 83

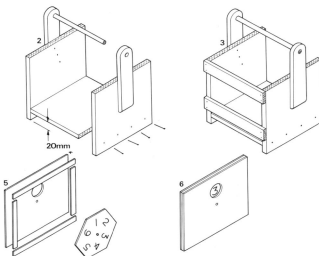

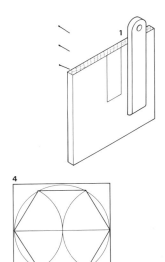

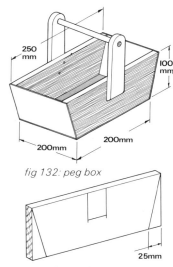

fig 131: stages in making
milk-bottle container

fig 132: peg box

fig 133: marking out a peg
box side

than the hexagon to allow it to be rotated freely. The numbers can be ready purchased stick-on figures which can be found in many stationery shops. The indicator is glued and pinned to the front of the holder: PINTS PLEASE is made up from ready-to-stick letters fitted in place after the holder has been painted.

A peg box

The photograph shows a box for carrying pegs when hanging wet clothes on a line. A larger version of this box would make a good 'trug' for holding small garden tools while working in a garden.

If the descriptions of the making of the other boxes have been followed you should have no difficulty in making the peg box. The handle supports must be glued as well as pinned to the box sides – pin from inside the box. Use a softwood for the sides and handle supports. Note that a slightly thicker plywood is used for the bottom and ends than in the other boxes.

Peg box

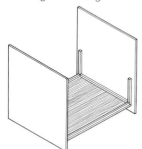

110mm

0mm

fig 134: first stage of making stool

fig 135: second stage of making stool

fig 136: third stage of making stool

fig 137: recess in stool to receive seat

8 Examples of work in chipboard

Sheets of chipboard are among the most easily available of wooden materials. Chipboard can be purchased uncoated in thicknesses mainly of 12 mm, 15 mm and 18 mm. It can also be purchased with a variety of applied surface coatings – plastic or wood. These coated chipboards are usually 15 mm thick, although 12 mm thick-coated chipboard can be purchased in some shops. The two common plastic coatings are either melamine (melamine formaldehyde) e.g., Contiplas, or vinyl (polyvinyl chloride or pvc) e.g., Target Panel. The common wood coatings are veneers of mahogany, teak or imitation teak. Coated chipboards can be readily purchased in a variety of board widths – 150 mm, 225 mm, 300 mm, 375 mm, 450 mm and 600 mm – with their long edges coated in addition to their top and bottom surfaces.

Iron-on edging strips

In order to cover freshly sawn or planed edges, strips of matching material can be purchased. These are made from wood or vinyl or from melamine with a glue coating on their backs. Under the action of heat from a hot iron, the glue melts into the chipboard edge which is being coated and forms a very strong bond. Vinyl edging needs to be ironed in place with brown paper between the hot iron and the edging strip.

A stool

A stool which can be easily and quickly made from faced chipboard is shown on page 76.
Stage 1. Glue and screw 15 mm square wood strips to the insides of both ends. The top edges of the ends need to be coated with matching ironed-on edging.
Stage 2. Glue and screw wood strips along the undersides of the seat and then glue and screw the seat to the wood strips already fixed to the ends.
Stage 3. Now screw the front and the back facings to the ends.

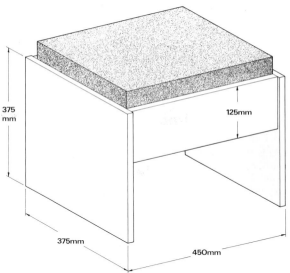

fig 138: coated chipboard stool

375 mm

125mm

375mm

450mm

Stool cushion cover ready to be sewn together

Final stages in the making of a loose stool seat

The cushion for this stool can be made from 75 mm thick polyurethane foam slab. An envelope of some furnishing material will need to be made to cover the foam block. Ask mother or sister to assist if necessary. One tip is to make the envelope a little smaller (about 5 mm each way) than the foam. Otherwise the material cover will tend to be loose around the foam.

Book shelves

Two types of book shelves are shown. Both are made in a similar manner, except that the edges of the end pieces of the standing rack are shaped, its shelves are sawn to

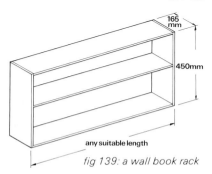

165 mm

450mm

any suitable length

fig 139: a wall book rack

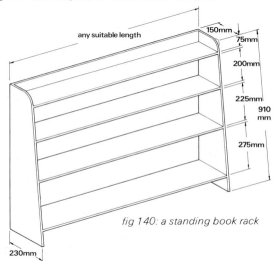

any suitable length

150mm

75mm

200mm

225mm

910 mm

275mm

230mm

fig 140: a standing book rack

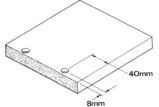

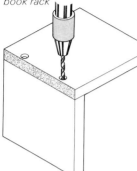

fig 141: first stage in jointing book rack

fig 142: second stage in jointing book rack

fig 143: third stage in jointing book rack

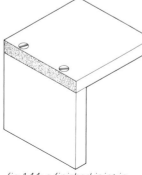

fig 144: a finished joint in book rack

different widths, and a back needs to be screwed to the top shelf. All shelves are joined to the ends with screwed joints – two screws to each join. The sizes of the wall rack are designed to enable it to accommodate only paper-backs.

Method of making

Stage 1. Mark the positions of screw holes in both end-pieces. Note that the holes must be set at least 40 mm in from the edges. If a smaller distance is chosen, the ends of the chipboard in which the plugs are driven may tend to split towards the edges. Bore the screw holes – 5 mm diameter and countersunk to receive the heads of gauge 8 screws.

Stage 2. Place each of the shelves in position under the pieces and mark each joint in turn by passing a rotating 5 mm drill through the screw holes in the end-pieces to mark positions for the Rawlplug holes in the shelves.

Stage 3. Drill 5 mm holes into the shelf ends to the depth of the length of the Rawlplugs being used: 30 mm. Glue fibre plugs into the holes. Plastic plugs are equally suitable.

Stage 4. Before screwing the book racks together, some edges will need to be coated with matching edging strip.

Standing book rack – white and teak 'Target' vinyl-coated chipboard

A corner of the wall book rack

A method of jointing the shelves of a book rack made from chipboard

fig 145: jointing central partition of table

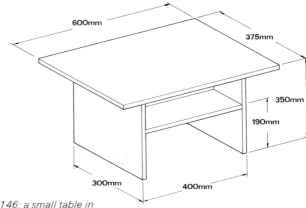

fig 146: a small table in
chipboard

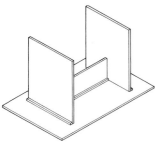

fig 147: jointing ends of table

A small table

Again, some form of coated chipboard is suitable for this piece of work. Don't worry about the screw heads showing on the outsides of the ends. The ends of the top overhang the uprights and this means that the screw heads will probably not be visible when the table is used. If you can afford them, use brass screws.

Stage 1. Screw (and glue) 15 mm square wood strips in position to take the stiffening rail and the uprights.

Stage 2. Screw the ends in place after marking Rawlplug holes and gluing the plugs in position in the ends of the stiffening rail and the shelf.

Stage 3. Glue and screw the shelf to the ends and also screw from under the shelf into the stiffening rail.

The edges of the ends of the top will need to be coated with matching edging strip.

A blanket chest

A blanket chest of simple construction is shown on page 77. The construction is based upon all adjacent parts being joined with 15 mm square wood strips screwed (and glued) into the corners. A photograph of a chest of slightly different design, but of similar construction, is shown.

Stage 1. First glue and screw wood strips to the bottom and to the ends. Then glue and screw through these strips into the back and front. Remember to saw out (using a coping saw) a handle grip hole in the front.

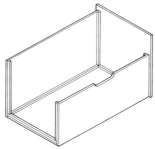

fig 148: method of jointing
blanket chest box

83

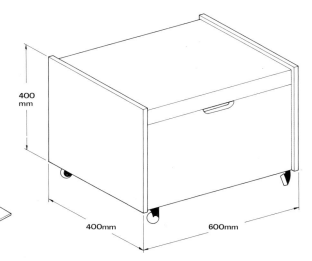

fig 149: a blanket chest in chipboard

400 mm

400mm   600mm

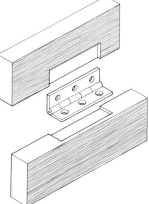

fig 150: method of jointing top of blanket chest

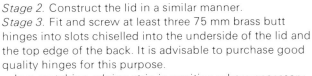

Stage 2. Construct the lid in a similar manner.
Stage 3. Fit and screw at least three 75 mm brass butt hinges into slots chiselled into the underside of the lid and the top edge of the back. It is advisable to purchase good quality hinges for this purpose.

Iron matching edging strip in position where necessary. Castors of the 'Easyglide' type should be screwed under each bottom corner to allow the blanket chest to be moved easily from place to place in a bedroom.

fig 151: hinging lid of blanket chest

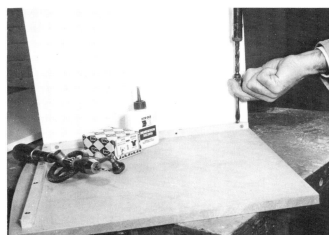

The method of jointing the corners of the blanket chest

fig 152: bedside cabinet in
chipboard

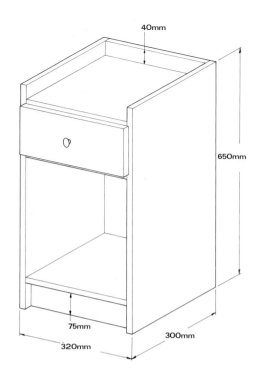

40mm

650mm

75mm

320mm

300mm

fig 153: method of jointing
bedside cabinet

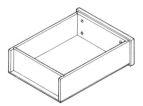

fig 154: method of construction of drawer of bedside
cabinet. See photo, page 80

A bedside cabinet

Stage 1. This cabinet is made by jointing with wooden
corner strips and with joint blocks. Wooden strips could be
used in place of the joint blocks.

Stage 2. The drawer box is made as described in the chapter
on constructions. An overhanging chipboard drawer front is
screwed in place from the rear of the front piece of the box.
A plywood bottom is glued and pinned under the drawer
box.

Great care is required to make sure the box exactly fits
and slides between its 'runners' inside the cabinet. Careful
planing and sanding of the glued-up box will assist in
ensuring a good running fit before the box is screwed to its
drawer front. Candle wax rubbed along the sides of the box
and on the top and bottom running edges assists smooth
movement of a drawer.

85

9 Some other examples of woodworking

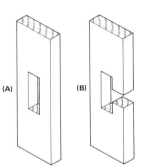

(A)   (B)

fig 155: (A) 1 piece:
120 mm × 36 mm × 12 mm
hole 36 mm × 12 mm
(B) 2 pieces:
120 mm × 36 mm × 12 m̃m
hole 36 mm × 12 mm
slot 12 mm × 12 mm

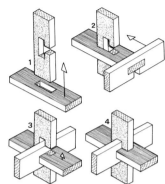

fig 156: fitting the parts of the puzzle to each other

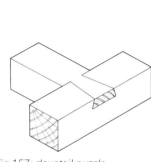

fig 157: dovetail puzzle

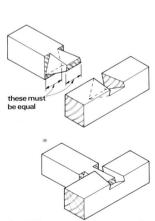

these must be equal

fig 158: secret of the dovetail puzzle

Wood puzzles

Making wood joint puzzles is an interesting woodworking activity. There are many such puzzles which can be made. Only two examples are shown here. These are of a simple nature, being comparatively easy to make provided that care is taken in cutting each part accurately. If they are badly made you will puzzle nobody with them. The idea is to produce joints which look as if they are impossible to assemble or take apart. The first consists of three pieces of wood with holes cut in them as shown in the drawing. The holes and slots must be accurately cut. Look at drawings (1) to (4) to see how the puzzle is assembled. Pass it to a friend and ask him to take it to pieces. When he fails to do so, quickly take it apart yourself and ask him to put it together. I very much doubt if he will succeed either way.

The dovetail puzzle joint demands very exact working. When assembled it appears to be a practical impossibility to take the two pieces apart. Of course, as you can see, the secret lies in sliding them apart along the line of the bottom of the groove. Note that two parts of the join must be exactly equal if the puzzle is to work successfully. Use wood that is square – say 45 mm or 50 mm square. But – people will only be puzzled if it is precisely made.

A wood puzzle

The wood puzzle taken apart

Place-mats and rack

Excellent table place-mats can be made from plywood which has been veneered on one side with a layer of Formica-type plastic laminate. Plastic laminate is tough, waterproof, scratch resistant and easy to clean. The plywood holds the laminate flat. Small pieces of plywood and off-cuts of laminate are often available quite cheaply from many shops. Some of the shapes in which the mats can be made are shown in the drawings. You should be able to design others. Those in the photograph on page 65 are 100 mm and 150 mm squares with each corner curved on a radius of 25 mm. Dimensions for these mats will depend on the sizes of the plates and containers you wish to stand on them. So measure these before you work the mats.

Method of making mats

(1) Saw and shape the pieces of plywood.

(2) Saw the laminate approximately to shape. It will cut quite well with fine toothed wood saws although the teeth do tend to get blunt. A hacksaw is better if you possess one Plastic laminate can also be cut by scoring its upper surface with a steel point and then breaking along the scored line across the edge of a table.

(3) Glue the laminate to the plywood. A good glue would be an impact glue such as Evostik or Bostik — remember to follow the maker's instructions. Cascamite glue could be used, but the mats then need to be placed under weights such as a pile of books, until the glue sets. In any case the glue must be waterproof because the mats will need to be washed on occasions.

(4) Trim the edges of the laminate to the shape of the plywood and clean them with sandpaper. Bevel the laminate edges at about 60 degrees with sandpaper.

fig 159: different shapes for table-mats

fig 160: shaping an edge of laminated plastic

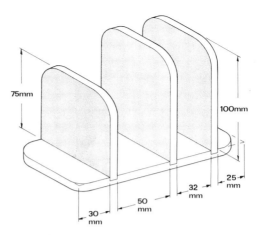

fig 161: rack for table-mats

75mm

100mm

25 mm

32 mm

50 mm

30 mm

Method of making the rack

The sizes to which the rack is made will depend upon the sizes of the mats you make. Choose a hardwood for this piece of work. The cutting of grooves into which the uprights fit has been explained in the chapter on construction. Shape the uprights and base after cutting the grooves and clean up each piece with sandpaper before gluing the four parts to each other. The housings may be nailed from underneath if you think it necessary, but do punch the nail heads under the surface of the wood. You do not want the nail heads to scratch a polished table top. Felt glued under the base will also prevent such damage occurring.

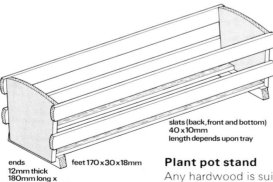

slats (back, front and bottom)
40 x 10mm
length depends upon tray

ends
12mm thick
180mm long x
150 tapering to 130mm

feet 170 x 30 x 18mm

fig 162: plant-pot stand

Plant pot stand

Any hardwood is suitable for this stand. It is designed to hold potted plants for standing on a table or on a window sill. This particular stand will hold three or four pots. Its measurements can be altered if you wish. A plastic tray is fitted in the bottom of the stand to catch excess water when

fig 163: feet to bottom slats

fig 164: feet to ends

fig 165: jointing of plant-pot stand

the plants are watered. It is advisable to buy such a tray and make the stand to measurements suitable to receive the tray.

You will require the following pieces of wood:

2 ends	180 mm by 150 mm by 12 mm
2 feet	170 mm by 30 mm by 18 mm
2 bottom slats	600 mm by 40 mm by 10 mm
4 slats for sides	640 mm by 40 mm by 10 mm

Screws and glue.

The given dimensions make no allowance for waste.

Method of making

Stage 1. Saw the two feet to shape. Saw the two bottom slats to exact length. Bore two screw holes at each end and screw the slats to the top of the feet. Use brass screws.

Stage 2. Bore holes in the feet and screw them against the insides of the ends.

Stage 3. Screw the slats to back and front. Use brass screws. The screw heads will look quite decorative if driven home with care.

Two coats of clear polyurethane varnish provide a good waterproof finish for the stand.

Coffee table with tiled top

Glazed, patterned tiles will provide good surfaces for coffee-table tops. Such tiles are decorative, heat resistant, waterproof and easily cleaned. They are also easy to lay on chipboard or thick plywood with tile cement as sold by the suppliers of tiles. Two tables of different construction are shown. The first is simple to make, yet strong. The second employs mortises and tenons. The second table frame

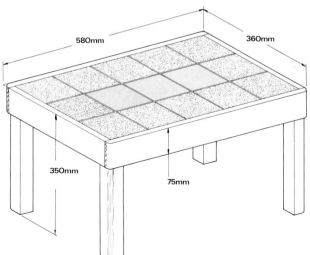

fig 166: small table with tiled top

89

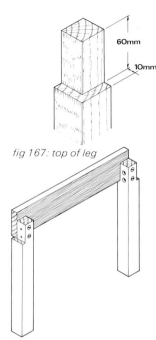

fig 167: top of leg

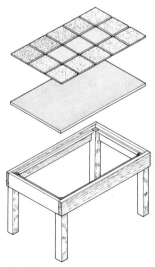

fig 168: first stage of making table; two end frames

fig 169: second stage of making table and its top

requires some skill to produce and unless you have made mortises and tenons before, it would be as well if you practised the joint before commencing to make the table. When making table frames, remember to check for squareness in all directions as the work proceeds.

Making the table – first type

Use a hardwood. You will need the following pieces of wood. No allowances have been made for waste.

4 legs	330 mm by	35 mm by 35 mm
2 rails	580 mm by	75 mm by 15 mm
2 rails	330 mm by	75 mm by 15 mm
1 top	550 mm by 330 mm by 12 mm chipboard (or plywood)	
2 support strips	510 mm by	15 mm by 15 mm
2 support strips	290 mm by	15 mm by 15 mm

Screws and glue.

Method of making – first stage

(1) Spread the tiles out in the pattern you wish to adopt. Allow 2 or 3 mm gap between each tile. Measure the overall length and width of the resulting rectangle of tiles. This will give you the exact size of the table top.

(2) Mark out and saw the top end of each leg as in the drawing. Bore 5 mm screw holes.

(3) Saw each rail to its finished length. Check for squareness.

(4) Glue and screw the short end rails into their recesses in the legs. Screw from inside the legs.

(5) Glue and screw the long rails to the legs from inside.

(6) Glue and screw the top support strips inside the rails. Check that they are at the table top thickness below the rail top edges. You can see their positions in the illustration.

(7) Saw out and fit the chipboard top to the frame. Do not screw it to the frame at this stage.

Making the top – second stage

(1) With the aid of a piece of scrap wood spread a thin layer of tile cement all over the surface of the chipboard top. Set the tiles in this cement. Check that the tops of the tiles are flat each way with a straight strip of wood or with a ruler.

(2) Place the table top to one side until the cement has set hard. While you are waiting, you could give the frame its first brush coat of clear polyurethane varnish.

(3) When the cement has set, work tile grouting into the spaces between the tiles. Tile cement thinned with water can be used. Wipe the surface with a damp rag and set

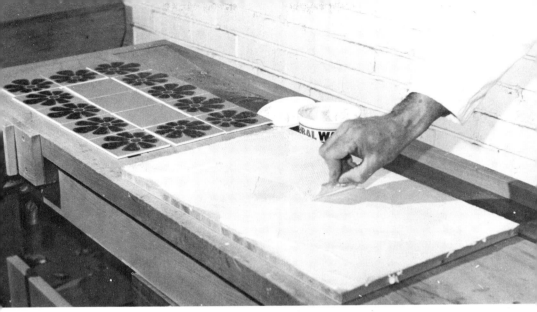

*Spreading tile cement before
laying tiles on table top*

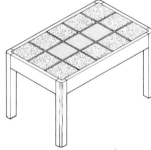

*fig 170: tiled top fitted to a
jointed table*

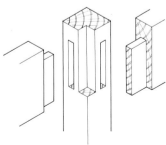

*fig 171: jointing for mortised
and tenoned table*

aside to dry. The second coat of varnish can be applied to
the frame at this stage.

Fixing the top

The top is screwed to the table from underneath through
the strips fixed to the rails. It is not necessary to glue as
well.

Method of making table – second type

For this construction use rails made from wood finishing
22 mm thick. This means the rail lengths, including tenons,
will be 566 mm and 346 mm long and the table will finish
594 mm long by 374 mm wide.

Cut the mortises and tenons as described in the chapter
on constructions. When the jointing is complete, glue up
the two end frames, allow the glue to set, then glue the two
long rails to the end frames. The top is fitted in the same
way as is the top of the first type of table except that it will
be necessary to cut notches in the legs on their inside
corners. The drawing shows this detail.

10 Fitting shelves

When other people discover your interest in working with wood, there is one job you are bound to be asked to undertake. This is the fixing of shelves either into an existing cupboard or into an alcove in a room or against a wall. The simple methods shown here depend upon screwing bearers against the inside of the cupboard or against the walls. The shelves are rested on the bearers. The bearers can be made from strips of wood averaging about 30 mm wide by 12 mm thick, thinner for lightweight shelving, heavier for shelves which are to carry heavy loads. When fitting shelves it is most important to try to get their surfaces level. This can be achieved either with the aid of a spirit-level or by measuring up from the bottom of a cupboard or from a floor to ensure that not only are both ends of the shelves at the same height, but that each bearer is also level. If a shelf is not horizontal, it will always look wrong and items placed on it may roll or fall off.

Shelves can be made from boards of solid' wood, from thick plywood or from chipboard. The shelf thickness depends upon the weight the shelf is expected to carry. Long shelves, particularly if made from chipboard, can be strengthened by screwing strips of wood edgeways on, either centrally or at back and front of the underside of the shelf.

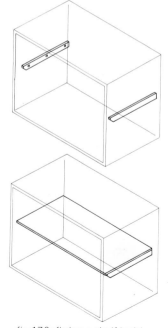

fig 172: fitting a shelf inside a cupboard (A) fitting bearers (B) shelf placed on bearers

Fitting a shelf in a cupboard

To fit a shelf into an existing cupboard, first mark the positions of the top edges of the shelf-bearers against the inside ends of the cupboard. Saw the bearer strips to length, shape their front ends, bore screw holes at about 100 mm intervals and screw the strips in position. Saw the shelf to size and drop it in place on its bearers. It is often quite unnecessary to fix the shelf permanently to the bearers, but if you think it desirable, spots of glue along the bearers will suffice. Place weights (books will do) on the shelf until the glue sets.

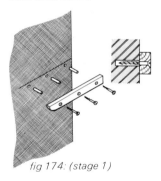

fig 173: shelves fitted against walls in an alcove

Fitting shelves in an alcove

Two methods of fixing shelves into an alcove in a room are shown. The quickest results are achieved by screwing bearers directly to the wall into wall plugs such as fibre or plastic Rawlplugs. Mark the shelf positions on the walls with a pencil, checking to make quite certain your two lines are level in both directions. Saw the bearers to length, shape the front ends and bore screw holes at about 100 mm spacings. Place each bearer in turn against the walls with their top edges lined up to the pencil marks. Mark through the screw holes to locate the plug hole positions on the walls. Bore the plug holes in the walls with a wall drill of the correct gauge for the plugs – a Master Mason or a Rawlplug drill are necessary for such wall drilling. Do not use wood drills, they will quickly become blunt and damaged. Insert wall plugs into the holes and trim their ends level with the wall surface with a chisel. Now the bearers can be screwed to the walls. Gauge 8 or 10 screws

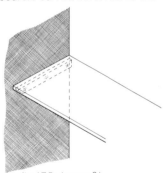

fig 174: (stage 1)

fig 175: (stage 2)

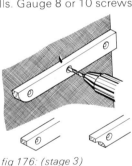

fig 176: (stage 3)

fig 177: (stage 4)

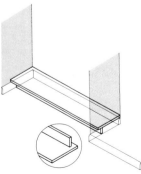

fig 178: fitting shelves in an alcove, a second method (stage 1)

fig 179: fitting shelves in an alcove (stage 2)

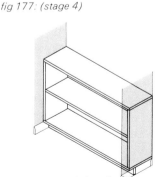

fig 180: fitting shelves in an alcove (stage 3)

93

are suitable for most shelves. The screws should be inserted between 25 mm and 40 mm into the walls. Don't underestimate the strength of this method of wall fixing – it is quite incredibly strong considering the size of the wall plugs. Properly fitted wall plugs will take the weight of a man. Saw the shelves to length and place them on the bearers. If permanent fixing is required, screw the shelves on to their bearers.

A second method of fitting shelves into an alcove which does not require the boring of holes into walls is shown. A bottom shelf is fitted on to the existing room skirting board. A plinth of skirting board width can be screwed under this shelf. Place upright boards of shelf width with bearers screwed against their surfaces on the ends of this bottom shelf. Other shelves are then positioned on the bearers and a top shelf placed on the upper ends of the uprights. If each shelf is a good, tight fit, this whole construction will hold together under its own weight. It can, however, be screwed together if thought necessary.

Shelves on brackets

Shelves in garages, sheds or workrooms can be fixed by means of simple brackets made as shown in the drawing by gluing and nailing strips of wood together. These brackets can be used in pairs – one each end of a shelf – or at one end only, the other end being supported on a wall-bearer. Shelves must be screwed to the brackets to prevent the shelf sliding from them. The brackets are screwed against the walls via wall plugs.

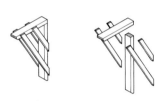

fig 181: a bracket for a shelf

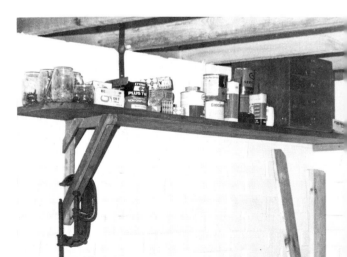

Shelf fitted into a corner of a workshop

Index

Page numbers in brackets ( ) indicate illustrations